Endor

"This book provides a real-world case study for all who want to understand the complex links between convictions, difficulties, God-centeredness, perseverance and success. The timeless principles illustrated in the book will change your life."

—Ebenezer A. Oladimeji, Ph.D.
President, Funnel Consulting LLC

"A transformational read showcasing a true walk of faith in a faithless world. The depth and personal stories can be related to by everyone facing daily challenges and looking for a way out ..."

—Akingbade Akinfenwa
CEO, ZEISTMASTER

"I am always amazed by the things that happen in the life of my friend, Eric Tangumonkem. His story of daily guidance and miracles from God serve as a good reminder to all of us that it is possible to see God work in miraculous ways in our daily lives."

—Pastor Joe Slaughter
Sr. Pastor at New Generation Community Fellowship
Dallas/Fort Worth Area

"This book is an immense expression of the audacity of faith. It takes faith to consider ones debt, which is even more than that of a whole community normal; it takes faith not to work because the law forbids one and yet one is in a precarious situation. In this book Dr. Eric Tangumonkem *is* inviting everyone in despondency to put their loads and intricate situations on God's shoulder and maintain an individual communication with Him."

—Nanche Billa Robert
Assistant Lecturer
Department of Social Sciences for Development
University of Maroua

"I enthusiastically recommend *Coming to America: A Journey of Faith.*"

—Tony Musumba, Ph.D.
Assistant Professor of Physics
Bismarck State College, North Dakota

"Eric's story is a powerful example of learning to walk by faith. I believe anyone who reads this book will be encouraged to trust the Lord to a much greater capacity and will be convicted of their little faith. The Christian life is truly meant to be an amazing adventure of faith, and Eric has modeled it. Read the book!"

—Pastor Bruce Cargile
Senior Pastor of Creekside Baptist Church
Richardson, Texas

"This book is a compelling testimony of the triumph of faith and obedience. As the late Dr. Martyn Lloyd Jones put it 'faith is obedient action to what God says.' Even so, Dr. Charles Stanley enjoins us to 'obey God and leave all the consequences to Him.'

"My friend Eric demonstrates the veracity of both principles in this remarkable treatise. I know many who will benefit from reading this book, and there are yet many who would be brought to repentance, and renewed faith by observing the ideas set forth herein."

—Julius N. Esunge, Ph.D.
Hope Outreach International Ministries

"What Eric has accomplished is truly phenomenal! It is a modern-day realization of the American Dream that happened against all odds, and is an inspiration to all. It is a beautiful story of Christian faith in action that serves as an example of what can be achieved if we deeply believe. Highly recommended!"

—Mike Liseser
Geologist, Denbury Resources Plano, Texas

"A wonderful and captivating story of Eric's journey from Cameroon to America. His story is a beautiful example of what can be if you believe. It is a must read!"

—Witney Shelley
VP-HR, Denbury Resources Plano, Texas

COMING
TO
AMERICA

A JOURNEY OF FAITH

DR. ERIC
TANGUMONKEM

IEM PRESS
Inspire, Motivate & Equip

IEM PRESS is honored to present this title with the author. The views expressed or implied in this work are those of the author. IEM Press provides our imprint seal representing design excellence, creative content and high quality production. To learn more about IEM Press visit www.iempublishing.com.

Unless otherwise noted, all Scriptures are taken from the *Holy Bible, New International Version*®, *NIV*®. Copyright © 1973, 1978, 1984, 2011 by Biblica, Inc.™ Used by permission of Zondervan. All rights reserved worldwide. www.zondervan.com

ISBN 13: 978-0-9916-2250-4
Library of Congress Catalog Card Number: 2014934214

CONTENTS

FOREWORD

ON FRIDAY, AUGUST 16, 2002, I met Dr. Eric Tangumonkem in the international student office at the University of Texas at Dallas apartment. We struck a friendship during our first week of classes and our friendship has grown over time. I have had the good fortune of seeing Eric and Elizabeth's beautiful family blossom in the last ten years. This story is a testimony of what God can do.

Eric came to the United States in very extraordinary circumstances. He traveled alone to the U.S. when his newborn baby, Afaamboma, was only a few months old. His wife and Afaamboma remained in Cameroon during his first year in Dallas, as he sought to further his education and advance his career. These were difficult times for Eric, but he persevered and trusted the Lord to open doors for his family to join him.

"God is taking care" has been the rallying cry for Eric in bountiful times and in tough times. The pressures of life have not abated, but his trust in the Lord has stayed strong. The book of Psalms says of the righteous man:

"That person is like a tree planted by streams of water, which yields its fruit in season and whose leaf does not wither. Whatever he does prospers."

—Psalm 1:3

This is a true story of how God has led and continues to lead the Tangumonkem family in these challenging times. In these tough economic times we need a remainder that;

"It is written: 'Man shall not live on bread alone, but on every word that comes from the mouth of God.'"

—Matthew 4:4

I enthusiastically recommend *Coming to America: A Journey of Faith.*

Dr. Tony Musumba
Assistant Professor of Physics
Bismarck State College
North Dakota, USA

ACKNOWLEDGMENTS

I THANK GOD for making it possible for this book to be written. Without Him working through us, the account recorded in this book would not have been realized.

Writing a book is not one man's job; it has taken the efforts of many people to realize this project. First, I offer sincere thanks and gratitude to my wife, Elizabeth Tangumonkem, for encouragement, constructive criticism, and for letting me say it as it happened.

I am grateful to my mother, Celine Lekunze, and dad, Abraham Lekunze, for instilling the fear of God in me at an early age, praying for me daily, and for demonstrating a life of faith before us.

Many thanks to all the teachers and mentors who have impacted my life over the years, and especially to Pastor Bisong David for being there for me at my hour of greatest need.

Special gratitude goes to Dr. James Carter, my mentor, for proofreading and editing the manuscript, and encouraging me to complete this project.

I also want to thank all of my friends who allowed God to work through them for the account recorded in this book to be made possible.

Finally, due to unforeseen circumstances the winepress team dropped the ball on this project and without the dedication and commitment of the team at IEM Press, this book would not have been published; thank you for a job well done.

CHAPTER 1

WHY I WROTE THIS BOOK

I will extol the LORD at all times; His praise
will always be on my lips.

—Psalm 34:1

EVER SINCE I landed in the United States of America, the most frequent question people ask me is; "Why did you come to America?" This is followed by, "Why the city of Dallas, Texas?" And then by, "Why the University of Texas at Dallas?" These are excellent questions that need answers. This book attempts to answer these and other questions to the best of my ability.

I believe God asked me to come to America to pursue graduate studies at the University of Texas at Dallas as part of the preparation to fulfill His purpose and calling for my life, the call to extend God's kingdom on earth by inspiring, equipping, and motivating others to reach their God-given potential.

This testimony is not about me and my family. It is about what God has done and continues to do in our lives. It is in keeping with the promise that we made to God that we will proclaim His wonders and handiwork on the mountaintops when He does them. What better way to do so than putting this in a book?

1

This is my side of the story, with the permission of my better half, Elizabeth, the mother of our four children. She is preparing to tell her own side of the story in the next book: *Living in America: A Journey of Faith.*

Above all, God alone deserves all the praise. He alone is to be worshiped and all the honor must be ascribed to him. Only then can we overcome the devil, for it is written:

> They triumphed over him by the blood of the Lamb and by the word of their testimony; they did not love their lives so much as to shrink from death.
>
> —Revelation 12:11

Note that this verse says the word of their testimony made them overcome the devil. This is made possible because testifying gives God the glory and removes the focus from us and puts it on Him. One of the greatest benefits for us is that our faith is strengthened, for we know the source of our victory is God and not us. Armed with this understanding, you will be able to overcome whatever challenge that may come your way. For you know that victory does not depend on you, but on God.

I am not testifying because I have everything in order; I am testifying because God's answer to our prayers does not depend on us. That is why the Bible says:

> Elijah was a human being, even as we are. He prayed earnestly that it would not rain, and it did not rain on the land for three and a half years. Again he prayed, and the heavens gave rain, and the earth produced its crops.
>
> —James 5:17–18

God is faithful and will back His word irrespective of what we think about it. His promises to us are "yea" and "amen." God has and will always keep His promises. You can count on them. These promises are the only sure foundation upon which you can build.

I am going to take you on a journey of my personal walk of faith with the Lord and will let you hear a firsthand account of some of the difficulties, questions, and challenges I faced and how the Lord brought me through them.

I state emphatically that God is alive and still answers prayers. He may not answer our prayers in the manner we want. He may not even answer them within the time frame we want. Delays do not change the fact that God is involved in every aspect of our lives and is almighty, all powerful, and able to do all He has promised.

God's word is infallible and it is the basis of our faith. It is the sure rock on which we stand, the compass that guides us, the currency with which we can tap into His resources. Without God's word our faith is just wishful thinking, and wishful thinking can only take us so far. Therefore, everything we do must be deep-rooted in Scripture and not on what is popular or necessarily makes sense to us.

We have our five senses to connect to the physical world. Our five senses have their place in our day-to-day lives. But mankind is body, soul and spirit. The only way the spirit-man can come alive in us is through faith in our Lord Jesus Christ. When this faith transaction takes place, Jesus Christ comes to live in and through us, making living by faith an essential aspect of our lives.

> I have been crucified with Christ and I no longer live, but Christ lives in me. The life I live in the body, I live by faith in the Son of God, who loved me and gave himself for me.
> —Galatians 2:20

Therefore, our walk of faith is not based solely on *our* ability, but on the faith of Christ, who lives in us. We follow the promptings of the Holy Spirit and take one step after the other. After all, God does not always show us the complete picture. He paints one part, followed by

3

the next and the next. Our faith walk is a work in progress and calls for continued abiding and trusting in Him.

We never say we have arrived, at least based on my experience. The Lord keeps rocking my boat and nudging me forward. This process is exciting and scary at the same time. I usually compare it to the children of Israel eating bitter herbs and goat meat on the night of the first Passover. It is bitter and sweet at the same time. What you focus on will determine your way forward.

You may decide to focus on the "bitter" part of the things in your life you consider bad and undesirable. The result is a life full of regret, resentment, ungratefulness, anger, bitterness, etc. The most appropriate thing to do is to realize that there is more than a silver lining behind every dark cloud. God is involved in every aspect of our lives and has everything under His control. Therefore, instead of dwelling on the negative things, you can choose to focus on all the wonderful things you have been blessed with, despite the dark storms raging around you.

I have come to understand that God did not only answer the prayers of the prophets of old, He is still interested in answering our prayers if we will be willing to pray and wait on Him to answer them in the way He deems fit and not place God in a particular box or set timetable. Let God be God and every obstacle will become a stepping stone to the next level.

You may be skeptical about what I am saying, but I encourage you to,

"Ask, and you will receive, seek and you will find, knock and the door will be opened to you." For everyone who asks receives; the one who seeks finds; and to the one who knocks, the door will be opened.
—Matthew 7:7–8

At each point before making any decision our motives have to be searched and the word of the Lord has to guide and lead us, even in our seeking and asking. When we understand the will of God and align with it, our prayers will be answered for we are praying God's will and are now in partnership with Him.

When God leads, He is surely going to provide. The essence of this testimony is to stress the importance of developing a close relationship with our Father in Heaven and an understanding that He is interested in the very minute details of our lives.

> "Are not two sparrows sold for a penny? Yet not one of them will fall to the ground outside your Father's care. And even the very hairs of your head are all numbered. So don't be afraid; you are worth more than many sparrows."
> —Matthew 10:29–31

For us to walk in victory we must first understand that God values us and would do with us what each and every one of us does with our most treasured possession; that is, care for and protect it at all costs. God was in the caring and protection business long before you were formed in your mother's womb. Therefore, He can do a far superior job of caring for and taking care of you more than your best effort can. The following verse puts it beautifully:

> Many, LORD my God, are the wonders you have done, the things you planned for us. None can compare with you; were I to speak and tell of your deeds, they would be too many to declare.
> —Psalm 40:5

What an excellent reminder of the great things God has already done and planned for us. Therefore, we can trust Him as we embark on this great journey of life. We know that no matter where life takes us provision has already been made for our sustenance and success. Yes, you can become who God created you to be. Obstacles, no matter how challenging they may be, are not enough to prevent God's plan for your life from being fulfilled.

This understanding prompted me to get aboard a plane bound for the United States of America with a small suitcase and very little money in order to embark on a project that needed thousands of dollars.

I invite you to follow me on this bittersweet journey and you will be blessed. Whatever your own personal journey is, with the Lord on your side, you are going to make it. Keep believing, trusting, obeying, and hoping.

You may already be wondering when we are going to get into the story. I will not keep you waiting any longer. The story now begins. Put on your seatbelt for a ride of a lifetime.

CHAPTER 2

KNOWING
MY FATHER
IN HEAVEN

Yet to all who did receive Him, to those who believed in his name, He gave the right to become children of God.
—John 1:12

THE JOURNEY OF a thousand miles begins with a single step. My journey to America began with the initial step of accepting Christ as my personal Savior and the subsequent deepening of my faith over the years. This laid the foundation of my personal walk of faith. Accepting Jesus Christ as my personal Lord and Savior is one of the most important decisions I ever made, and it has literally shaped and influenced my worldview in a way that nothing else has or could.

When I was eleven years old, I attended an evangelistic crusade organized by the Mumdani Believers Association in Bamumbu village part of the then Fontem subdivision of South West province Cameroon. The Gospel message preached by Reverend Solomon Kemamah exhorted us to turn from our sinful ways and accept God's forgiveness.

The evangelist stressed that sin is dangerous because it brings separation between us and our Father in heaven. Furthermore, if this separation is not corrected we will be separated from our heavenly

Father throughout all eternity. This separation in itself is terrible, and the place we will live forever is called hell. Hell is a terrible place, a lake of unquenchable fire and torment without any hope of escape.

Finally, the evangelist offered some hope, a way of being reconciled to our Father in heaven. I was made to understand that our heavenly Father created hell for the devil and all his demons and not for us. But if we choose to remain in sin, we will continue to be separated from Him. I was convicted by the Holy Spirit of my sinfulness and separation from my Father in Heaven.

> For all have sinned and fall short of the glory of God, and all are justified freely by His grace through the redemption that came by Christ Jesus.
>
> —Romans 3:23–24

You may be wondering what type of sins an eleven-year-old was convicted of. I was guilty of the following: telling lies, stealing, envy, anger, selfishness, disobedience to my parents, and the list can go on and on. Let me spare you all of the details.

Despite the awful feeling of my depravity and emptiness, I was made to understand that my Father in heaven wants to have a relationship with me, and that He loved me so much that He sent His Son to come and die on the cross for me. There was no need for me to do anything apart from accepting that I was a sinner, asking God to forgive my sins, and inviting Christ to come into my life. I did just that and invited Christ to come into my life as my Lord and Savior.

I was led in the sinner's prayer of repentance, but I did not feel anything different afterward, except that I knew that my sins had been forgiven and that I was now a child of God. The next day we were told that God wants to empower us through the baptism of the Holy Spirit. All of us who had just asked Jesus Christ to come to our hearts, and other believers who were interested in the baptism of the Holy Spirit, were instructed on the importance of, and the need to be filled by the Holy Spirit.

We were all gathered in a room at the Fon's Palace in Bamumbu, and the pastors, leaders and all who were filled with the Holy Spirit started praying for us. They moved from one person to another laying on hands and asking God to fill us with the Holy Spirit. Those praying for us were all speaking in languages that we could not understand. The praying went on for some time, and I suddenly felt like electricity went through my entire body and I burst into unknown tongues also. And what a joy that flooded my soul that day.

My dad was also in the crowd, but did not speak in tongues. He was finally baptized by the Holy Spirit some years later. As far as I am concerned, receiving the in-filling of the Holy Spirit with the physical manifestation of speaking in tongues had nothing to do with me. I asked the Lord for the Holy Spirit; He gave me and that is all I can say at the moment.

Now that I have let "the cat out of the bag," so to speak, do not drop this book because you disagree with speaking in tongues or the manifestation of the gifts of the Holy Spirit. The Lord is going to bless and strengthen your faith if you keep reading. I am telling my story and am doing all I can to be as accurate and detailed as possible.

After all, we are not our own. We have been bought at a price and God is the one to receive all the glory and praise for everything that happens in our lives. Let me repeat that you should not look at me, but Jesus Christ, for all what I am writing about was done by Him and Him alone. It has nothing to do with me, but everything to do with Jesus Christ working through me over the years.

After the Holy Spirit baptism, as it was called, I was taken to the river and baptized that same day. The denomination I was raised in is called the Full Gospel Mission and they do not believe in infant baptism.

Therefore, some objected to me being baptized, even though I was eleven years old and no longer an infant. But some of the elders said that since I was already baptized by the Holy Spirit, there was no reason that I should be refused the water baptism. This is how I became the first to be baptized amongst my seven siblings. All my other siblings have accepted Christ as their personal Savior and have all been baptized and are faithfully serving the Lord.

Immediately, I came out of the river, I had the first test of what this walk of faith was going to look like. The crusade was moved to another location and we all had to move there. In my infant zeal and enthusiasm, I told the person I was having a conversation with that, "Somebody hit me on my cheek and I turned the other cheek." Immediately it occurred to me that I had lied, and I told the person that I had lied and that I was very sorry about it. I also confessed my sin to God and asked for His forgiveness.

Even though I had asked for forgiveness, I had this nagging feeling that I was doomed and that God was not going to accept me again. How can it be that I was baptized by the Holy Spirit and had just come out of water baptism and have lied? It was later on that I understood that the devil, the enemy of my soul, was discouraging me and wanted me to remain in condemnation even after I had confessed my sin to God.

I have since learned that our Father in heaven is gracious and will forgive our sins if we acknowledge them and confess them to Him. As you can see immediately, this account is not by any means an account of somebody who has everything in order. I am a man of passions like you.

But our focus is not just going to be on our failures and weakness or the besetting sin in our lives. We have to rise above that and pursue the Lord. We do not have to look far to see the Lord, for our body is the temple of God. He comes to live in us when we invite Him to come into our lives.

Through this incident I learned a very valuable lesson. We must not allow the devil to prevent us from having fellowship with our Father in heaven because of false guilt from sin. We must confess our sins and accept God's forgiveness immediately when we realize we have sinned.

If restitution has to be done, then do it immediately. This will put an end to the accusations of the devil and the false guilt associated with these accusations.

I also learned that any feelings of condemnation and unworthiness are from the devil and they have to be dealt with it accordingly. When we sin, the Holy Spirit will convict us, but will not condemn us. Instead, the Holy Spirit will nudge us towards God's forgiveness and restoration. Our walk of faith depends on a proper understanding and application of this truth.

The more we use our muscles the stronger they become and the more proficient we get at using them. Our faith also must be exercised and we have to learn to trust God in an incremental fashion and also give God the glory in all circumstances at all times. The reason for this is that if we do not give God the credit for the things we consider small, we will not do so when greater things happen.

The greatest danger of not realizing that God is involved in even the small things is that we begin to think that we are in charge and when something big comes our way, it will be very difficult for us to believe God will step in and deliver us. In my case, as was that of King David, I have realized that I can trust the Lord to do greater things in my life when I recall some of the past "small victories":

> But David said to Saul, "Your servant has been keeping his father's sheep. When a lion or a bear came and carried off a sheep from the flock, I went after it, struck it and rescued the sheep from its mouth. When it turned on me, I seized it by its hair, struck it and killed it. Your servant has killed both the lion and the bear; this uncircumcised Philistine will be like one of them, because he has defied the armies of the living God. The LORD who rescued me from the paw of the lion and the paw of the bear will rescue me from the hand of this Philistine." Saul said to David, "Go, and the LORD be with you."
> —1 Samuel 17:34–37

Here David recounts how he killed a lion and a bear at the same time, acknowledging that in both cases God was the one who delivered him from these animals. It is important to note that David was not the only shepherd in Israel who rescued his sheep from lions and bears. Israel had many shepherds, and attacks from hungry bears and lions trying to snatch a sheep for a meal were common.

Therefore, one can assume that most of the soldiers who were facing Goliath had at one point or another encountered a lion or a bear and had been able to deliver their sheep from certain death. But why did none of the soldiers draw inspiration from this seemingly small victory when faced by the greater challenge posed by Goliath the giant? The answer is that they thought deliverance from a bear and a lion was something within their power and God had little or nothing to do with it.

Their victory had no faith component, since it is natural for a lion or a bear to attack sheep and for the shepherd to chase the lion or the bear away. So what is the big deal? There is no need to thank God for it. No wonder all these men trembled and could not stand up to the challenge from Goliath the giant.

Then enters David, who had a very different understanding of what others considered the mundane. Instead of saying "I delivered," he said that God delivered him from the lion and the bear. That is why, when faced with a far greater challenge from Goliath, he faced the giant with the same understanding that the God who had delivered him before was going to deliver him again.

There is usually a big chasm between the natural and the supernatural, and choosing to see God at work in both realms is the only way to bridge both worlds, for God is the God of all.

Therefore, the nature of the problem does not matter, for our Father in heaven is bigger than any challenge we have faced, are facing, or will ever face. My first step was accepting that my Father in heaven had forgiven my sins. The next step was to believe what the word teaches:

What, then, shall we say in response to these things? If God is for us, who can be against us? He who did not spare his own Son, but gave him up for us all—how will He not also, along with him, graciously give us all things?

—Romans 8:31–32

There are many instances in the past when God answered specific requests that I made. For example, while I was at the University of Buea in Cameroon I completely ran out of money and had no food at home. I was living about three miles from the University campus so, I had to trek to school and back each day.

On my way back on one particular day, I told the Lord that I had come to the end of myself and that I was going to borrow some money if He, God, did not do something about my situation. I needed money and food. I went to the house of one of our church elders to borrow some money, but when I got there, I felt I should not borrow anything from him.

After some time, I left his house and went home. Close to midnight I heard a knock on my door. I got up and opened the door and could not believe that my dad was standing in front of me. He had left our village (more than 165 miles from where I was attending university) to come to the Delegation of Education for some transaction, since he was a school headmaster. I was not expecting him, and it was a great relief that he showed up without notice at my greatest hour of need. My dad's coming was an answer to prayer, for he never visited me again during the more than three years that I spent at the University of Buea. I could not go home during vacation because it was too expensive, and only got to go to the village after completing my undergraduate degree.

On this one and only occasion that my dad visited me, he came with some money and I was able to buy some food. Despite the fact that my dad was there, he could not solve all of my problems. I had a fever and chest pain a couple of days before his arrival, and was coughing up mucus mixed with blood. I went to the hospital and the doctor recommended a chest X-ray. I could not afford to get the X-ray and just had to depend on my heavenly Father to heal me. I was healed; if not this testimony would not have been written by me. All of this took place on December 3, 1996.

I learned that my earthly father is limited and that my heavenly Father has the ability to take care of me. This understanding changed my life and my focus moved from trusting and depending on my dad to a new understanding of my heavenly Father's boundless ability and resources.

You may be wondering what I was doing in school without food and money. About a year or more prior to this I had applied to get into the geology program at the University of Buea for a Bachelor of Science degree without sufficient funds for my tuition and boarding. My family was going through economic hardship at that time. This caused me to stay at home without going to school for one year after graduating from Government High School Mbengwi, with two advanced-level papers in geology and biology.

The fact that we were going through economic difficulties did not mean that my dream of acquiring a university education had to die completely. Dreams can be temporarily put on hold, but should not be allowed to wither. You have to keep your eyes on the goal and keep the dream alive by doing all you can with what you have, while waiting for the appropriate moment to move forward.

Consider all setbacks as opportunities for refinement, refocusing, and strategizing. Remember nothing is wasted in God's economy. Even the momentary setbacks will definitely yield great dividends for you if you do not allow the momentary pain associated with the setback to overwhelm you.

While waiting, you have to occupy yourself with activities that are in line with your dream, until the condition is ripe for the next season. It is important to take a close look at whatever resources, talents and abilities you have and make the most of them. This will mitigate the overwhelming sense of failure and defeat that may want to swamp you and completely choke life out of your dream. The fact that you are not going where you initially set out to go does not mean that you wonder around aimlessly when faced with roadblocks.

My roadblock was the lack of funds to enroll in a university program immediately after high school graduation. I did not allow the lack of funds to prevent me from being productive while I waited for the appropriate time to go back to school.

My family has been baking bread since I was a kid, and we all participated in the baking. I mixed and baked my first dough when I was about nine years old and continued thereafter.

Therefore the most natural thing for me to do during the year I was at home was to bake bread. In addition to baking, I grew tomatoes and a variety of vegetables. In addition to gardening, I bought and sold other wares in order to raise some money. I could not save much because Cameroon was going through an economic crisis and at one point salaries were slashed by more than 50%. An already precarious situation was compounded by a devaluation of the currency. Therefore, most of the money raised through my business activities was spent helping to take care of our family.

Despite all of these challenges I had the conviction to go to the university and get a degree in geology. One week before classes were to begin, I told my dad that I was ready to go to school. He said my admission letter had not yet arrived. I told him I was going to be admitted, so he gave me part of my fees and transportation from the village to the city where I was going to attend the university.

I gathered whatever belongings I had and put them into a small suitcase and left the village. On the way I became disturbed. Questions were running through my mind. Where was I going to sleep? What was I going to eat? How was I going to take care of myself? How was I going to pay my tuition? The questions went on and on. I had every reason in the world to worry, based on the circumstance surrounding me.

The money I had with me was not enough to take care of my registration, let alone rent and food. All of these questions were running through my mind as I sat in the bus that was heading to Buea, the city where the university was located. To overcome my worries and anxiety, I took out my Bible and started reading, meditating, and praying. Then the Lord made a very strong impression in my heart through the following verses of Scripture in the book of Proverbs:

> Trust in the LORD with all your heart and lean not on your own understanding; in all your ways submit to Him, and He will make your paths straight. Do not be wise in your own eyes; fear the LORD and shun evil.
>
> —Proverbs 3:5–7

The words in these verses literally struck me in an unusual way and spoke to me personally. I was made to realize that my understanding of my circumstances, though real, was not the only reality. Yes, I was not financially viable, but I had to go past that understanding and put my trust in the Lord, for He is able to take care of me. After pondering and meditating on these verses for some time, I had peace and assurance that God was going to see me through my undergraduate program. As you will discover, I then went through three and a half years of great difficulties.

Today I am very grateful that the Lord counted me worthy to go through all of the experiences that I went through during the three and half years that I spent at the University of Buea. I learned to depend on the Lord for everything and realized that my background, race or color cannot place any limitations on me. I am a child of the King, and I am seated with Christ in the heavenly places. Therefore, I can do all things through Christ who strengthens me.

It is very easy to let our backgrounds trap us if we fail to understand that God is the equalizer. I was born into the royal family of the Bamumbu people. My dad, being one of the hundreds of princes and princesses fathered by my grandfather, who had at least a hundred and five wives, did not have much to show for being a prince.

After my grandfather passed on to join his forefathers, one of my uncles was crowned king. And, as the tradition stipulates, he who becomes king inherits all. This means that all of the other princes and princesses are left without any inheritance. They literally have to fend for themselves after their dad went to meet his forefathers.

Bamumbu is nested on the top of what used to be a volcanic mountain, but a series of cataclysmic and extremely violent eruptions blew off the top of the mountain and created a huge horseshoe-shape depression called a caldera. This particular caldera is characterized by deep valleys, ravines, steep hills and cliff faces, volcanic plugs, and mountains. This makes it one of the most rugged terrains in the country and the only habitable caldera on the Cameroon Volcanic Line.

My ancestors moved to and settled in the caldera because it offered natural defenses and protection from other warring ethnic groups. My people named the area Mbu, which means "cave" in the Mundani language. When the first colonialists from Europe came in contact with my people, they changed the name to Bamumbu. Contact with Europeans meant that the kingdom, like many other surrounding kingdoms and kingdoms all over Africa, lost its sovereignty. Exasperatingly, these independent people were grouped into new nations, with a lot of negative consequences.

Personally, the way to move forward is to focus on what God is doing right now and to trust Him to bring closure to some of the negative fallouts of colonialism and neo-colonialism. The economic hardship we were going through in Cameroon was a result of the Structural Adjustment Program implemented by the International Monetary Fund (IMF) and the World Bank. This program was geared towards poverty reduction, but brought untold suffering and misery on the people of Cameroon and other African countries. The Structural Adjustment Program involved; slashing salaries by 50%, devaluing our currency, cutting educational, agricultural, and other subsides. This proposed remedy worked well on paper, but when implemented became a recipe for suffering and misery for an already vulnerable people.

Enough complaining about the damage and misery brought on my people by outsiders. Complaining can only take one so far. We did not only inherit problems, we inherited the good news of salvation, formal education, and many other things. We can choose to complain and blame all we want when faced with unfair and difficult circumstances. Or we can choose to become an agent of change and encouragement; after all, complaining alone will not change our situation.

I started writing letters to encourage my parents not to be too worried, for God was taking care of me. I must say here that I have wonderful parents who loved their children so much and were ready to do anything for me and my other siblings. In fact, they did all in their power to take care of us. But at this particular time they could only do so much.

I am so proud of Mum and Dad for all of the sacrifices they made to send me and two of my siblings to an excellent Roman Catholic boarding school, Our Lady Seat of Wisdom College in Fontem, which is owned and operated by the Focolare Movement, a Roman Catholic international organization. This organization operates in 182 countries and was founded by Chiara Lubich in Trento, Italy, in 1943. This educational institution laid a solid foundation for us and exposed us to people from other parts of the world. My English teacher was from England, my religion teacher from Scotland, Chemistry teacher from France, Math teacher from Madagascar, French teacher from former Zaire, Physics teacher from Germany, and Geography teacher from Cameroon, just to name a few. Meeting and interacting with people from all of these different countries made me increased my cultural intelligence quotient. This is just one out of the many good qualities this educational institution had. Above all, the school provided a safe and secured environment for us to excel in our studies.

My elder brother, Godson, and my younger brother, James, and I graduated from this school with ten subjects each in the General Certificate of Education Examination (GCE/OL). During this time, having four subjects was considered a pass and the maximum number of subject was ten. We did well, thanks to the extra mile our parents went. I would never trade them for other parents even if I had the opportunity to choose.

Talking of sacrificing, it is difficult to describe what my parents had to go through to pay our tuition, room, and board. It is a miracle that they were able to do it. Things were tough, and I remember Mum breaking down one day and crying after we ate and asked for more food, and there was nothing for her to give us.

In all of these trials and difficulties, I came to accept who I was. I came to terms with my background. After all, I was not consulted before being born in Africa, to particular parents in a particular village and at a particular point in time. I began to see that my heavenly Father had the final say and that my background, no matter what it is, cannot prevent Him from accomplishing His purpose in my life. What freedom and liberation this understanding brought to me. Envy and wishing to be somebody else quickly lost its grip on me and I became much more determined to succeed in whatever I set my heart on.

Instead of moving away from God, I was drawn closer to my heavenly Father and my trust and dependence on Him deepened over the years. One may be tempted to say that I had no choice than to trust God since I was having a lot of difficulties. This assumption is not true, because I had a very close friend I walked to the university with each day, and his greatest obstacle to coming to faith in Jesus Christ was the fact that his life was very difficult.

He kept asking me why a good and benevolent God would allow some people to live in affluence while others, like us, live in poverty. My friend complained and was not very open to hearing what I had to tell him, for he kept asking, "How can a good God allow so much suffering on Earth?" I told him that we were suffering because Adam and Eve chose to believe the lies of the devil in the Garden of Eden, thereby disobeying God.

The result was that they died spiritually and became separated from God. All creation also became impacted by this act of disobedience.

19

Since we are descendants of Adam and Eve, we are born in sin and our only hope is salvation through Jesus Christ. We must acknowledge our sins, repent from them, and accept the forgiveness in the blood of our Lord Jesus Christ.

As you would expect, my explanation did not do much good. I am still wrapping my mind around this issue of suffering, but have come to understand that the sin of Adam and Eve is the root cause of our suffering and that of the natural world. God had to take on our humanity in the person of our Lord Jesus Christ in order to solve this problem. Therefore, I can trust Him because He shares in our suffering. The issue of suffering should not prevent anybody from accepting Jesus Christ as their Lord and Savior. Poverty, oppression, and natural calamities should not discourage us from seeing the love of God in all circumstances and at all times.

Intellectual prowess, riches, and material possessions also can be a major stumbling block to many. I had very rich friends who lived on the university campus and were not subjected to trekking three miles to school as some of us were. They had electricity, clean water, money, and a never-ending food supply. Humanly speaking, they had it all. As such, they did not see any reason to believe in God. To them religion was for those who are feeble minded, irrational, unpolished, uneducated, frustrated, poor, needy, and not adequately clothed.

It was not difficult for them to ask, "Why should I pray when I already have the answer? Why should I pray when reason and brain power can provide all the answers?" I made them to understand that prayer is more than asking for stuff from God. It is about having a conversation with our heavenly Father. He speaks to us through His word when we read it and we in turn speak to Him through prayer.

They would tell me, "Pastor," as I was nicknamed then, "leave us alone to enjoy our life. You are missing the good things of life. We are too young for religion and may someday consider it when we get older, but now is the time to pursue the pleasures of life."

They could not understand why I was so passionate about sharing my faith and encouraging them to yield their lives to the Lord Jesus Christ. I strongly condemned cheating in exams, corruption in the public services, cohabitation, and other vices. As we are going to see, the time of testing came for me.

Talk is cheap. But actions speak louder than words. Talking "the" talk and not walking "the" walk is worse than wishful thinking and will not do us any good. It will turn us into hypocrites, and cause our faith to become stagnant. Faith is exercised each time talking is followed by the right action. This happens because if we believe in a cause strongly enough we will act on it. When we act on less important issues we will be able to act on more important issues when the time comes.

I have come to the understanding that the best way to know my Father in heaven is by believing and acting on His word. His word is powerful and alive and the more I believe and trust Him the more I see His hand upon my life. This is not a one time deal, it is a lifestyle, as you are soon going to discover.

CHAPTER 3

EVER-INCREASING FAITH

"Consequently, faith comes from hearing the message, and the message is heard through the word about Christ."
—Romans 10:17

L IFE IS NOT lived in a vacuum, we are faced by diverse challenges and our faith is strengthened as we overcome one challenge after another. The challenge may be financial, as it was in my case, but your own may be something very different. The end result of whatever you may be dealing with is that your faith will be strengthened, and that you will learn and get better and better at walking by faith.

Whatever dream you have will require time for your faith to grow and mature. This growth process, and whatever way God chooses to do it, varies from individual to individual. That is why there is no point in wishing to be somebody else. You are you and unique in the way God created you. Take the case of Moses; he had the dream to free his people from slavery and bondage under Pharaoh, the tyrannical ruler of Egypt. After killing an Egyptian slave driver, he fled from Egypt and took care of sheep for forty years in the land of Midian. Before being led by God after the dramatic burning bush experience to come back and fulfill his dream of freeing his people. Whatever stage you are in your dream, know that God is taking care of you and that you will make it.

All in all, I experienced God's provision and answer to prayer in many different ways. On those occasions when I was left with little or no money, the Lord would provide miraculously. For example, on October 20, 1996, I had to go to Mutengene, a different city from where I was living, to attend a meeting organized by the Mumdani Believers Association and I had no money for my taxi fare. I went home after church, and when it was very close to the departure time God brought someone to buy tomatoes seedlings for 100 frs CFA (CFA stands for *Communauté Financière Africaine* (African Financial Community), (100 frs was about 14 cents).

I had grown a few tomatoes seeds to plants by the wall of my room, and they were doing well. There was no plan to sell any, but I had to when somebody suddenly showed up and offered to buy some. The 100 frs CFA I got from this stranger was not enough to pay my fare to the meeting, for the normal fare was 150 frs CFA.

I took the money, prayed for favor, and then went to the road, stopped a taxi, and told the driver I had only 100 frs CFA instead of the usual 150 frs CFA and the driver accepted. I attended the meeting and God provided, through the brethren, for me to pay my way back. I am getting into all of these details to let you see that my trust and dependence on God was a gradual process and I had to slowly learn to pray for everything. I wrote down some of these things and have selected a few of many to share with you for your encouragement.

On February 26, 1996, I was standing in a line in front of the dean's office to sign up for classes for the semester. The university regulations stipulate that students cannot take more than 18 credit hours per semester. I needed to take 19 credits that semester and I shared that information with those I was standing in the line with. They said doing that would be impossible, for the dean was very stern. In fact, as we were still standing there, those who went ahead of me came back and said they had tried to sign up for more than 18 credits but were turned down.

My turn came and I went in and told the dean that I needed to take 19 credits for the semester. He hesitated and asked me why. I explained to him that it would enable me to graduate on time. He let me sign up for the 19 credit hours. This may be rationalized away by saying it was just luck on my part. And you may be wondering why this particular incidence is important.

I learned then that the heart of kings is in the hands of the Lord. This particular lesson came in handy when I moved to the United States of America for graduate studies. The second lesson I learned was never to let people to talk me out of what the Lord was about to do in my life. I have heard it many times: "You do not have what it takes. It cannot be done. It is impossible. There is no way out." The list can go on and on, but there is no need to dwell on it. The Word of God squarely addresses all these negatives and any other ones that will be concocted. He is the God of all impossibilities and knows no limitations.

On another occasion, when I was in year two at the university, things became very difficult financially and I was not able to pay my rent of 2,000 frs CFA (about $3 then). The average rent for apartments close to the university campus was about 8,000 frs CFA (about $12). Remember, I left home without enough money and no bedding or cooking utensils. So I had to stay in a single bedroom with my aunt for the first few weeks, while trying to register. We had neither running water nor electricity and were living in very close quarters and sharing the same bed.

Aunt Magdalene is my mum's younger sister and many years older than me. She was doing what was expected: taking care of her sister's son. It was an extra mile on her part, for her room was roughly three meters by three meters. Her bed occupied most of the room, and the remaining space was taken by her pots and pans. Cooking was done on a little stove close to the door, and at times in front of the house on the veranda. There was no table and no space to put one. Studying under such circumstances was not feasible, and I had to do something quickly about my situation.

Mile 16 Bolifamba, where my aunty lived, was a farming community with a single tarred road that ran through it. All of the other streets that crisscrossed the community were not tarred and became a sea of mud after heavy rainfall. Most of the houses were wooden houses and a few concrete houses dotted here and there. The few students who lived there were from not well-to-do backgrounds. Some of these students had no sponsors and kept themselves in school with the money they raised doing odd jobs during the holiday.

After careful consideration, I felt that it would not be a wise thing for me to stay in Mile 16 Bolifamba, but there was nothing I could do to change my situation. That was when I met a friend who lived close to the university, and he offered to share his room and bunk bed with me. Things went well initially, but by the end of the semester the relationship turned sour because of political differences and our approach to one particular witchcraft-related incident.

Both of us were from the same ethnic group and a well-to-do uncle of mine occasionally gave us money to take care of some of our expenses. Since my uncle was a member of the ruling political party, it was common practice for the government to ask top ranking civil servants working for the government to go out and campaign for the ruling party. These top ranking officials would in turn solicit the help of others to spread the message of the party in power.

When I was asked to participate, I turned down the offer because the political machinery put in place by the government had not helped the country. It had ensured that one political party completely dominated the political landscape and, as the old adage goes, "Power corrupts and absolute power corrupts absolutely." Prior to elections you hear politicians telling the man on the street, "Scratch my back and I will scratch yours." The backs of the people are scratched by offering them a few bottles of beer in exchange for their votes.

The implication is that the people indirectly sell their right to ask the politician tough questions and are unable to hold their leaders accountable. I was of the opinion that the playing field should be leveled for everybody. That is, good laws should be passed so that the people who were subsistent farmers could get a good price for their produce. They would then use their hard-earned money and buy all the beer they wanted and not be forced to vote without asking the hard questions. My position did not sit well with my uncle and he blacklisted me. My friend had to choose between maintaining his relationship with my uncle and keeping me in his house.

This was a tough decision for him to make, and I made things more difficult for him by being the only one who stood up to support a student accused of practicing witchcraft in our hostel when all the other students were demanding the expulsion of the "wizard." What started as a rumor slowly ballooned to the "truth." One of the law students living in our hostel was declared a wizard and a trial was set up for him.

We all gathered in the equivalent of the leasing center, and the trial began with the accused student in absentia. I immediately made a motion that the trail should be stopped because the accused was not present. The unanimous response of the other students was that since the accused student was absent it was proof that he was guilty. I tried to make them understand that there are a thousand and one reasons for the student's absence, and that he might have just been running late. The other students were not willing to listen; the trail had to go ahead as planned.

One student after the other gave reasons why they believed the student in question was a wizard. Some said he was behaving in a strange way; others said they saw him in their dreams behaving in a bizarre manner.

I raised my hand one more time and said, "We do not have the right to try this student and there is no evidence to prove that the student under trial is a wizard." But I was hushed by the other students; some even used the Bible to justify their position by saying, "Suffer not the witch to live." Instead of seeking for the death of the student, a lesser punishment was pronounced.

It was unanimously agreed by the other students that the accused student be asked to leave the hostel with all of his belongings that night and should never set foot there again. I still objected to this. What they were asking the student to do was impossible, unfair, unjust, and inhumane. Some of the students were delegated to deliver and enforce the judgment, and things got out of control and the police got involved. The student finally left the hostel, but did not do it in the way that had been stipulated. Due to the police intervention, the student was given enough time to look for new accommodation somewhere else and then moved all of his belongings.

The position I took made me unpopular. I was accused of being rude and inconsiderate, and of showing off. This incident, my political stand, and other similar situations cost me my accommodation. My roommate was kind enough to let me stay with him until the end of the first semester, but then I was dropped like a hot potato. This meant that I had to look for new accommodation, and since it was expensive to live close to the university campus, my only option was to look for cheap accommodation somewhere else.

The only place where I knew housing was cheap was where my aunt was living. I had to swallow my pride when I moved back, because my aunt did not approve of the first move that I had made.

Coming back meant that I was admitting failure and accepting that her judgment was correct. There wasn't much I could do with the little money I had. I moved back to Bolifamba, a farming community about three miles away from the university, and rented a single room in the same apartment complex in which my aunt was living. This time I had my own separate room, but it had no furniture, running water, or electricity. The room was very damp and during the rainy season the walls were completely covered by mold. My books, clothes, and other belongs were also ravaged by the mold.

This unhealthy living condition made me sick most of the time. I decided to move into a different accommodation. I rented a room from a family and the rent was 2,000 frs CFA ($2.80) per month. The house had no ceilings and the walls had a lot of holes, which easily let in mosquitoes. The buzzing and bites of these malaria-causing mosquitoes made it difficult to sleep at night.

Despite these challenges, I was blessed in that the house had electricity. This meant that instead of using a kerosene lantern to study, as was the case in the other house, my studies were done by the aid of a single light bulb in the room. With electricity I was able to concentrate better on my studies.

Also, by this time I had managed to get a bed, but the bed was too big for the mattress that I had. So I used my bed sheets to cover the empty part of the bed where there was no mattress. I stayed in the house for a semester and ran out of money completely. Fortunately for me, I had not signed a lease and was paying my rent on a monthly basis. A lease would have made my mobility very difficult. Running out of money meant I had to move again. Where was I to move to?

As I was contemplating what to do next, a friend told me that he had been offered a job to take care of some animals on a farm a mile further from where I was living. He told me the job came with free accommodation and I could take one of the rooms in the farmhouse and stay for free. Rent free accommodation? Wow! Praise the Lord, hallelujah! How could I turn down such an offer? What other options were available for me? I did not know of any other.

To me this was God-sent and I immediately moved my few belongings into the farmhouse. I did not really know what I was getting myself into until I settled into my new house. It seemed I had jumped from the frying pan into the fire! I went back to more than square zero. Up until now, I had the impression that my living condition was bad, but what I got into made all the other places that I had lived before seem very comfortable.

My new house was in the "bush" and there was no running water, nor electricity. We prepared our meals on an open fire under a tree, because our fuel source was firewood. I had to study using a lantern. At times

I could not, because there was no way to buy kerosene for the lamp. I was originally living at mile 16 Bolifamba, and the farmhouse was at mile 15 Bokova. This meant that I had an extra mile to cover to and from the university. This did not make my commute any easier at all.

Each morning, I would leave the house full of energy and sing as I walked to school. But by the end of a long and tiring day in school I was wishing my house was closer to the university campus. Indeed, it took the grace of God to walk back to the house in the evening. Most of the time I did so on an empty stomach, for living far from school meant that I could not go back to my house for lunch. Also, there wasn't enough money for me to buy lunch during the day.

Hunger was not the only problem I dealt with. A more serious threat was the highway I walked on to school daily. The highway was narrow, without any sidewalks, and had numerous potholes. In order to escape these potholes, some of the drivers drove dangerously close to the edge of the road, with disastrous consequences. For example, a friend got hit by a car once, but his life was spared. I had a few close calls, and I am grateful for God's protection.

It is only the grace of God that spared one from the recklessness of some of the drivers. This type of behavior was supposed to be checked by the forces of law and order, but they were part of the problem and not the solution. Most of the policemen were more interested in extorting money from the drivers than ensuring that the drivers were obeying traffic rules and that their vehicles were properly maintained.

Once in a while as we walked to school, we would argue about the proper way the policemen and the drivers should behave. Some were of the opinion that the drivers were victims of unscrupulous policemen, while others felt the drivers were to blame for being part of the problem. Most of the drivers carried more than the allowed number of passengers in their cars, thereby breaking the law. The law enforcement officers would not enforce the law and would take bribes from the drivers. These drivers carried extra passengers so that they would have extra money to give a bribe to the policeman. This became a vicious cycle with no possible end in sight. Who would break this seemingly impossible deadlock? Was there any way forward?

Rumors said that the policemen were instructed by their bosses to collect the money from the drivers and share it with them at the end of the day. Some of this money was expected to be sent up the chain of command to the "big man" at the top. Anybody who tried to disrupt the status quo risked their promotion. The fear of losing the personal benefits associated with maintaining the status quo kept things the way they were. We never did come to any conclusions concerning this issue, for we had more pressing issues to deal with. I was soon to move again for the fourth time in two years.

My friend lost his job on the farm just when the second semester of my second year was ending, so I moved back to mile 16 and a Christian couple (Uncle Daniel and Aunty Winnie Angaama as we fondly called them) gave me a room to stay with them in their house. What a blessing and answer to prayer. A free room was nothing short of a miracle, for I was financially hard up. This couple was very kind and they let me stay with them until I graduated from the university about a year and half later. During that time, I helped with the housecleaning and, when time permitted, in the kitchen. I mention this because cleaning the house was viewed in some circles as a woman's work, but I learned that God always uses what we have to move us to the next level. Cleaning the house did not make me less of a man. It blessed this wonderful couple that was gracious enough to offer me free accommodation.

Despite all that I was going through, the Lord was answering other prayers in my life and setting me up for the next move. As I said, we are a work-in-progress and will never say we have reached completion until we meet our Father when He calls us home. Therefore, consider whatever you are going through today as a stepping stone to your tomorrow. That is why the Bible says that we should not neglect the days of small beginnings:

"Who dares despise the day of small things, since the seven eyes of the LORD that range throughout the earth will rejoice when they see the chosen capstone in the hand of Zerubbabel?"

—Zechariah 4:10

While in Government High School Mbengwi, I attended the same church as my future spouse, Elizabeth Abek. Apart from attending the same church and the same high school, there was nothing else that we shared in common. We were not even friends.

She was raised in an entirely different part of the country from me and moved to where we attended high school because her elder sister was working there. She was in middle school and I was a senior, so I graduated before her and moved to a different city. It turned out that Buea, where I went for my undergraduate studies, is a few miles from where she was raised. This made it possible for our paths to cross again during my first year at the university.

I started praying for a spouse in high school and by the end of my first year at the university, the Holy Spirit impressed in my heart to ask for Elizabeth's hand in marriage. How this happened and all that transpired is the subject of another book that will soon be released, titled: *Getting Married: Our Journey of Faith*. But I bring this up to drive home the point that our walk with the Lord is a faith walk and every aspect of our lives, marriage included, has to be seen in that light.

I remember asking Elizabeth if she would wait for four years to get married to me. I also asked her to understand that after graduating with my bachelor's degree I was not guaranteed a job. Therefore, we would have to trust the Lord to perfect what He had started. We had great odds against us and only God could make it possible for us to get married. I have always told people that this is one of the craziest things I ever did.

Well, it was not entirely my project. My Father in heaven answered my prayer. I had been praying for a spouse who would accept me the way I was, not because of my financial or material status. I did not know the Lord's timing and when it finally came I obeyed. It was not easy on my part when I made the commitment to get married after four years. All we could do was to pray and wait.

I graduated and moved to the capital of Cameroon to do a master's at the University of Yoaunde I. Exactly four years from the time I proposed to my spouse we felt it was time for us to get married. As a student, I was making about 35,000 frs CFA a month, which by then was about $50. Our tradition recommended that I pay a dowry to my spouse's family, and we were also required to organize a traditional wedding ceremony, civil wedding, and a wedding in the church.

These different wedding ceremonies were going to cost hundreds of thousands of Francs. And, based on my meager resources at that time, it was an astronomical amount of money, a seemingly impossible obstacle to overcome. Notwithstanding, God provided and we got married on December 31, 2000, without going into debt. I could not believe my eyes that I was indeed married and I am still in awe each time I look at my wife. That is why our first son was to be named Afaamboma, which, when translated into English, means "God's work" or "the Lord's doing."

This was to act as a reminder for us of what the Lord had done. When we got back to the city, we discovered a few months later that we were going to have a baby and I was speechless. The nurse thought I was overjoyed. No! No! The daddy-to-be was scared of how he was going to take care of his young wife and new family.

I was still in school and my wife was also a student. We prayed that the Lord would provide and He did. First, James my younger brother, who was working at the time, was transferred to the city that we were living in, and he decided to move in with us. He paid the house rent while I took care of the utility bills. Second, our income multiplied by three times by the time Elizabeth had the baby. This happened through more opportunities for me to do tutoring. We also organized tutoring classes for college students in our living room. These classes succeeded because of the support my spouse gave me. Despite the fact that she was heavily pregnant she took it upon herself to teach some of the subjects.

She had to step in because I had my hands full, trying to teach biology, geography, religion, English, economics, and history to secondary school students who were preparing for the General Certificate of Education Examination. Each evening for more than three months our living room would be transformed into a classroom. We borrowed a few school desks from neighbors for the students to sit on.

Before class the furniture in the living room was taken out and replaced by the desks, which would be taken out at the end of the class. We were able to sit at least thirteen students in our living room. Despite these unfavorable conditions, most of the students were grateful for the extra tutoring we were offering.

Most of these students worked during the day and had not had what could be considered a normal school life, but they were determined to get an education and would not let anything stop them. They were survivalists, and greatly motivated men and women who wanted to better their lives. Their stories need to be told and their courage and determination has to be emulated by all facing difficulties.

Life in the city had many challenges, since accommodations were very expensive and we had to move into a house close to one of the marshes in the city. The house had no plumbing and the area was heavily infested with malaria-causing mosquitoes. This meant we were attacked frequently by malaria fever.

We began to pray that the Lord would open better doors for us. Above all His will for our lives would be done. As I walked on the streets of the city, I would see some women behind the wheel and would imagine the day I would be able to get my wife a car also. I would try to imagine how that would happen, but I could not see it in the physical. Instead, I saw her with the eyes of faith driving her own car. We started praying about starting a business so that our lives would get better. But I was still a student with little or no prospects of getting a job after graduation. In the midst of all these uncertainties, the Lord set in motion a series of events that was going to take me out of my homeland. God works in ways that do not necessarily fit in the box we want things to fit in.

The next time an opportunity presents itself before you and is more than your wildest imagination, do not get frozen in your tracks. Your boat is being rocked to loosen it from the shore so that you can move into deeper waters. Fear, worry, and anxiety are expected reactions, but do not allow them to prevent you from launching into the deep. Let us do that together as my dream of getting a graduate education in America unfolds.

CHAPTER 4

GO TO AMERICA

"For we live by faith, not by sight."
—2 Corinthians 5:7

M Y BOAT WAS going to be rocked beyond my ability to control it, and the next phase of my walk was going to be greater than anything I had experienced so far. Go to America for graduate studies! How did I ever in my wildest imagination come up with such an idea? As you will discover, it was not my idea and carrying it out also did not depend on me, for there was nothing to show for on my part. It was going to require a mustering of every iota of faith that was available to me, and my faith would be stretched beyond my wildest imagination.

I went to a conference organized by the Geologic Society of Africa in March 2001, at the Yaounde Congress Center, to present a poster on my master's thesis. I was mesmerized by the quality of the posters and presentations of the other geologists that came from the United States, Australia, Germany, and Great Britain, just to name a few of the countries that were represented there.

A light went on in me. I had an "Aha" moment and I felt I had to leave Cameroon for further studies. Immediately, when I got home, I told my wife that we had to pray for our way to America, for I felt the Lord was impressing in my heart to go to the U.S. for further studies.

I said we had to pray our way to the U.S. because we were expecting our first child and were nowhere near financially capable of accomplishing such an undertaking. The airfare alone was more than a million francs. The thought of a million francs ($2000) scared me. How on earth were we going to come up with such an enormous sum of money? In the physical this was an impossibility, an insurmountable mountain.

That is why, prior to this, all of my thoughts of going abroad were focused on Southern Africa. I had been hoping to go to South Africa to do a graduate degree in Geology at the University of the Witwatersrand, Johannesburg. Moreover, I had a cousin at the university who had promised to hand deliver an application package if I filled it out and mailed it to him.

In addition, it was humanly feasible in my mind, for I had heard stories of people who used public transportation to go to South Africa through Gabon, Congo, and Zimbabwe, and would get into South Africa through Botswana or Mozambique. I felt this was possible since it did not require flying and would not cost anything close to the millions that were needed to go the United States of America.

It had never crossed my mind to even think that I would ever go to the United States to study because America was too far from home, traveling there was too expensive, and tuition there was also expensive. The closest I got to thinking of going to any western country was Germany, because I was hoping to apply through the Deutscher Akademischer Austausch Dienst (DAAD) Scholarship Program. However, all of this speculation was going to come to an abrupt end and my faith would be stretched more than ever.

During the conference, I volunteered to pick up the foreign dignitaries at the airport and take them to their hotels. That is when I met Professor Mohamed Abdelsalam from the University of Texas at Dallas, in the United States of America. I took his contact information and sent an e-mail to him after the conference asking him to send an application package to me. I also requested an application from professors from a University in Honolulu and the University of Queensland in Australia.

All of these professors were kind enough to mail the requested admission information. After careful thought and prayer, we felt the Lord was leading me to go to the University of Texas at Dallas, so I completed the application and mailed it in. I applied only to this University and we prayed that if the Lord wanted me to go to the U.S., then my application would be accepted.

After a few months, the university sent a letter stating that my application had been received, but I had to take the TOEFL (Test of English as a Foreign Language) and the GRE (Graduate Record Examination). The tests cost $110 and $140, respectively. It was impossible for me to raise such an amount of money since our income at the time was barely enough to take care of our basic needs.

I told my spouse we would have to save meticulously over the course of a year to raise money for one of the exams. Therefore, it was going to take us two years to raise the money needed for me to register and take both exams. This was our first major roadblock and just one of many that we would have to overcome for me to travel to America.

My previous experiences had taught me that when God leads, the journey does not necessarily have to be easy or devoid of obstacles. We have an enemy, the devil, who would do all to oppose and if possible, derail the will of God in our lives. That is why we are admonished to be on the alert at all times:

> Be alert and of sober mind. Your enemy the devil prowls around like
> a roaring lion looking for someone to devour.
> —1 Peter 5:8

The enemy of our soul wants to devour our lives and will do all to try and prevent what the Lord wants to do in our lives. The good news is that we have been promised victory over the devil by God. For it does not matter how big the challenge is, God who lives in us is more than equal to the challenge.

All of the obstacles before us crumbled one after another as we marched forward in faith. The first breakthrough came through my mother, who through a series of miracles and divine connections was in the U.S. for a conference dealing with the empowerment of rural women. The Lord raised her up for a moment like this. I contacted her and asked if she would be able to pay the registration for the exams and she did.

We were overjoyed and praised the Lord for his goodness. I prepared for the exams, took them after three months, and sent in the results. About a year after I started the admission process, praise God, Hallelujah, we received an admission letter in the mail. We were ecstatic and overwhelmed with joy. At last our dream was about to come true. To God be all the glory and praise for answering our prayers.

My joy was to be short-lived. I had been hoping to get a scholarship or a teaching assistantship with the admission, but the admission letter stated that I would be responsible for my tuition and room and board. This meant we had an even greater mountain in front of us to climb. At that time, international students interested in attending the university of Texas at Dallas had to show proof of funds to the tune of $15,000. This would amount to 11 million francs CFA. This money had to be deposited in a bank and the bank statements sent to the university and the US Consulate in Cameroon for a student visa to be issued.

Here I was looking at a project that would cost many millions, but I did not even have a hundred thousand in the bank. We were completely overwhelmed by the magnitude of the obstacle in front of us. So we regrouped and promised our Father in heaven that if He made a way for me to travel, we would testify that He is alive and that He answers prayers.

The first thing that happened was a change in my language. I started talking to people about the millions needed for me to go to America. At first it brought ridicule and scorn from some quarters. I remember a cousin who said, "Man, you are very bold. If I wanted to travel abroad

I would not even consider America for it is very expensive to study there." My response was that God was taking care. When He leads, He always makes provision.

Another friend told me that he has never nursed the thought of going abroad to study, because he does not have any relations out there and does not want to have false hopes. To quote him, he said, "Man, you need a Moses to part the Red Sea for you." He was not far from the truth. We were at the shore of the Red Sea, or should I say the shore of the Atlantic Ocean, and needed a miracle.

We needed divine intervention and all we could do was pray. I shared with some well-to-do brethren in the church we were attending, but nothing fruitful came out of my request. I needed somebody who had enough money to provide a bank statement for me so that I could send it to the university. When the university received the bank statement they would then send the travel documents that I would take to the embassy for a visa to be issued to me. This crucial document is called an I-20. Without the I-20 from the University of Texas at Dallas I could not go to the embassy to try and get a student visa. I got desperate and a Muslim friend told me to come see his mum and explain my situation to her, for she might help. My spouse and I went, but the outcome was futile.

I called a well-to-do uncle and pleaded with him to help, but got a negative response. We were pushed to the wall and there was nothing else we could do. One day while my spouse and I were praying, our Father in heaven spoke through her in a word of prophecy that I was going to travel and that I should not be afraid. We became encouraged and energized, but were still at square zero. We had no bank statement to send to the university and nobody willing to help us with the bank statement that we badly needed.

Finally, after some agonizing months had gone by and when we had almost given up all hope, we had our breakthrough. The Lord moved in the heart of a family friend who asked her bank to issue a bank statement for me to send to the University of Texas at Dallas. I sent the bank statement and after one month my I-20 arrived. We had another victory lap. That was in June 2002.

I immediately set up an appointment at the U.S. Embassy in Yaounde, since my classes were supposed to start in fall 2002. My hope was to get a visa as soon as possible and travel towards the end of June. I reasoned that upon arrival in the U.S. I would have at least two months to work and make some money before starting school in August. I made all of these calculations based on misinformation and partial truths gathered from various people.

We all had this false notion that in the U.S. there are lots of jobs; for example, that washing dishes at restaurants or waiting tables would bring you tons of money. We were clueless about employment restrictions on international students and the challenges of living in America. As such, I would be in for a rude awakening when reality would later set in.

I went to the U.S. Embassy in June. I had to get up at 4:00 A.M. and was at the Embassy by 5:00 A.M. I stood in a long line and finally got in at 8:00 A.M. I was called by the consular officer for the interview and my heart started pounding. Why would my heart not pound? After all, many other people who had gone ahead of me had been denied visas. As such I did not know what to expect. But I knew what my Father in heaven had promised and that He was going to make a way.

After going through my documents, the consular officer said that everything looked okay, but he was suspicious of my bank statement. The bank statement issued to me was from a local banking institution. Therefore, the consular officer instructed me to go ask my sponsor to transfer the money into one of the international banks in the country. To say I was devastated by his request would be a gross understatement.

I was completely shattered to the extent that when I came out of the embassy building, I could not talk to my spouse and dad, who were waiting outside. It seems we had been offered the final blow and that nothing was going to salvage the situation. It is one thing for somebody to give their financial information to you and a completely different ball game to ask them to transfer their money into a different bank. I was speechless. So I decided to go to the Embassy a second time the next week to try again.

I got up early, went to the Embassy, and waited in the line for my turn. When I was called up a different person interviewed me and still asked me to go transfer the money into an international bank. I came out of the Embassy and wrote a letter to the university explaining my difficulties in getting a visa and they sent a letter to me, which arrived after two weeks. We were now in July. I went to the Embassy a third time and showed the consular the letter, but I was still turned down. I had exhausted all of my options and many people, even my siblings, were of the opinion that I should not keep straining myself by keeping false hope.

They suggested I give up. Towards the last week of July, God moved on our behalf and instead of transferring the money our family friend just went ahead and opened an account in my name. She put in 3 million francs of her own money and borrowed 5 million francs at 10% interest a month and added it into the account. Now I had 8 million francs, but I needed at least 11 million francs.

That is when a cousin suggested I contact my uncle again. He said that I should go to the city where my uncle lived, talk with him personally, and explain to him where I was in the process. I had already contacted my uncle a month before over the phone and he said it was not possible for him to offer me any help.

However, my cousin insisted that meeting him physically could be a game-changer. That is why I immediately went to the bus stop, bought a ticket, and travelled overnight to meet my uncle. My uncle was glad to see me and enquired about the reason of my visit. I told him how I was having difficulties securing funds that would enable me to travel to the U.S. for graduate studies.

The Lord granted me favor with my uncle and he gave me a bank statement worth 10 million francs. It is a miracle that he could come up with such an amount. He later told me after a few years that I was very lucky, for he had been keeping the money on behalf of other people and after that transaction the money was disbursed and he has not been able to get such a lump sum again. According to my uncle, my luck made it possible for me to get the bank statement. There is no such thing as luck; I believe God was meeting my need of a bank statement and anything short of recognizing that will be giving credit to the wrong quarters.

Now that I had enough money for the visa, I left the next day to Younde and went to the Embassy for the fourth time. I presented the 8 million francs bank statement that was in my name and the 10 million francs that my uncle had given me. I was very confident I was going to get the visa that day, since I now had proof of 18 million francs, which is more than the 11 or so million francs that was needed.

That day I met with the same consular officer who had interviewed me the first time, and he said I should come back the next week because the Embassy needed one week to investigate if the bank statements were legitimate. This was done routinely to curb fraudulent cases.

I went home and we kept praying. My dad told me to go to church on Sunday and testify that I was going to go to the U.S., since it was going to be my last Sunday in Cameroon. I had already booked my flight to travel on August 14th, for classes were expected to start on August 21st.

I went to church, the entire church prayed for me, and I informed the brethren I was travelling to America the following Saturday. I did not tell them I had not yet been given the visa. Therefore, a part of me was saying, "What are you going to tell these people if you go to the Embassy on Tuesday and you are denied a visa again?"

Well, I had already been to the U.S. Embassy many times and had been denied a visa each time. Some of my fear was neutralized by encouragement from my dad. Thank God for godly parents.

In fact, my fear was confirmed when I went to the Embassy on Tuesday, making it my fourth time. The same consular officer was assigned to interview me. He said, "You have been here multiple times and have proven incompetent to pay for your schooling in the United States of America."

I was shocked and dumbfounded. For he said I only had proof of 10 million francs and that I needed 11 million francs. A thousand and one questions rushed through my mind. For example, what happened to the other bank statement worth 8 million francs that was in my name? I did not even have photocopies to prove I had deposited bank statements worth 18 million francs.

I had the longest few seconds of my life as I tried to collect myself and decide what to say. Here was this man in front of me who had stopped my God-given dream of going to America. In an instant I realized that I must say something and whatever I had to say must be the right thing for that was my last chance.

In fact, based on his statement my case was closed. I had been at the Embassy too many times and did not have enough funds to show that I would be able to pay for my schooling in the U.S. Thank God that the right words were put into my mouth. I immediately told him that I had deposited two bank statements the week before and both of them together were worth 18 million francs.

He looked at me and said, "I believe you, go and pay for your visa fee." I can still feel the chills that I had on that day as I am writing this, even though it has been over seven years. I went and paid the visa fee and was instructed to come and pick up my visa for America on Friday. I went home and there was a lot of jubilation and praising God for granting me the visa.

Little did we know that the journey had just begun. The challenges ahead of us were going to be far greater than those we had already overcome. I had the visa to travel to America, but I did not have the money to pay for my flight, tuition, or room and board.

Our family friend who had opened the bank account in my name with partially borrowed money decided to lend me 3 million francs from the eight million that was in the bank. This was a miracle because I did not have any collateral security for such a sum of money to be given to me. And I will be forever grateful for her help.

It is worth noting here that my lack of money did not prevent me from pursuing my God-given dream of going to America for graduate studies. When I got the inspiration to go to America, I first of all believed it. I also acted upon it by applying for admission into an American university. Finally, I told people about what I was doing and expecting to happen in my life. In other words, I had done my due diligence to the best of my ability. I had presented what I wanted to do to the Lord with the expectation that He was going to use it and take me to the next step. Walking by faith does not mean you fold your arms and do nothing. There is a process involved and that is when action has to accompany what you believe and confess.

As you believe, confess, and act, your focus should be on God, since focusing on your resources and abilities or the lack thereof is deadly. Many dreams have died at inception because we focus on the lack of resources and the obstacles that oppose our onward match to fulfilling our dreams.

This should not be the case, for, if God is the initiator of the dream He will also make the dream come true. The timing and manner in which God chooses to make this happen is entirely left to Him. All you are required to do is believe and trust Him to lead you one step at a time. This is the one tried and true antidote that will put fear and unbelief out of business.

You may be wondering why you are having a hard time believing and trusting the promises of God concerning your life. And why walking by faith is so difficult and almost unattainable. Part of the challenge is that we try to measure our level of faith using our feelings. Most people say, "If I do not feel it, then it is not possible, it will not work." The command is not to allow our feelings to dictate our next move, but to believe the Lord and trust in Him. Do not allow your feelings alone to guide you.

I did not feel like leaving my spouse and young son and embarking on a journey without enough resources to accomplish the task that was ahead of me. My feelings told me it was not going to work and that

I would be disgraced and laughed at. In spite of all of these negative feelings, I got aboard a plane to the United States of America without enough money to pay for my schooling. What in the world was I thinking? Well, keep reading and you will find out. You have come with me thus far and I encourage you to keep going.

It was a daring move on our part to wed as students, without much to show for. Here we are cutting the cake and looking forward to our new life as a married couple.

Bamumbu Village, located in the interior of the Bamboutos caldera, where I was born and raised.

On my way to the Island to sell food and buy smoked fish and shrimp. I am standing on the rim of the canoe and the stuff to be sold is in front of me. The canoe was usually overloaded, making the journey more dangerous.

A street in Mile 16 Bolifamba, with its wooden houses and water puddles, which makes perfect conditions for mosquitoes to breed and transmit malaria. I lived in Mile 16 for three years while attending the University of Buea.

49

CHAPTER 5

AMERICA HERE
I COME

*"Now faith is confidence in what we hope for and assurance
about what we do not see."*
—Hebrews 11:1

I PACKED THE few belongings I had into a single small suitcase and got onto a KLM flight via Brussels on Saturday at 11:00 P.M., a day after I got my American visa. There was not enough time to say goodbye to everyone, and it was not easy leaving my spouse and ten-month-old son behind. Since I did not know when I would see them again, but I was comfortable getting onboard a plane to the U.S. without enough money to pay my tuition, and other expenses because I had learned to depend on my heavenly Father's provision. I had a lot of apprehension, for this was my first flight, I did not know anybody personally in the U.S., and I had just $2,000 American dollars on me. My tuition for the first semester was more than $4,000 and I still needed a couple thousand dollars for books, housing, and food.

The situation was compounded by the fact that the money for my flight and the balance that was on me was borrowed at 10% a month, making a total of 120% interest a year. The amount was 3 million francs. I was naïve to think that it was going to be easy to raise money in America and pay back this loan immediately. When I finally got to the U.S., reality set in. At the University of Texas at Dallas where I came to pursue graduate studies in geology, I was told international students are not allowed to work off campus and on campus jobs are difficult to get.

God still moves on our behalf when we are willing to step out in faith and trust Him. The process may not be very comfortable but we know that we can face tomorrow since He holds the future. All I did was pray. I finally landed at 4:00 P.M. on Sunday, August 11, 2002 at the DFW (Dallas-Fort Worth International Airport) and was expecting to see somebody with a sign containing my name but there was no one in sight. I scanned all the faces but there was nobody there who seemed to be expecting me. What was I to do? Is this what coming to America would entail?

I had just a single phone number on me and that was the phone number of a missionary, Dr. Duane Collins. He had been a missionary in Cameroon in the mid-'70s and had left the country many years ago. I had never met him. When I was seeking admission into the University of Texas at Dallas, I contacted him and he said he would be very happy to pick me up at the airport when I arrived.

The delays in obtaining a visa caused me to keep pushing my arrival date forward, and when I finally got the visa he was out-of-town, so my last e-mail to him indicating my arrival date and time never got to him. When I arrived at the airport he did not know I was even coming, let alone waiting for me. I tried to make a phone call, but did not know how to dial the pay phone.

There were instructions on how to dial the phone and I followed them, but the phone kept rejecting my coins. What was I doing wrong? I left Cameroon with a few dollar bills on me. When I arrived at the Dallas-Fort Worth International Airport, I tried to use the paper bills at the pay phone and it did not work. A lady at one of the check-in counters changed a few dollar bills and gave me some coins. My first American coins, and I had to learn a crash lesson on what the different

52

denominations were. Right now, I cannot re-call if the lady gave me quarters or dimes. From all indications, I was doing something wrong and would never be able get a hold of Dr. Collins.

There was a sea of people around me, but nobody seemed to notice me. Didn't they know that I was new here and needed help? What was I to do? God help me get through this. By divine providence, an African-American man walked by and I told him that I was having difficulties using the pay phone. The man seemed not to be in a hurry as all the other people were. He handed his cell phone to me and showed me how to use it. At last the solution to my problem was at hand.

A lot of things ran through my mind as I dialed Dr. Collins' number. Maybe he was somewhere in the airport and had forgotten to bring a sign with my name on it. Or he had forgotten I was coming. I was not ready for what I was about to hear.

Remember, Dr. Collins and I had never met, so my heavy Cameroonian accent did not help the situation when I got him on the phone. He said that he was in Oklahoma at the moment and asked if I knew any other person. I said I did not, and that he was my only contact. We were having a hard time understanding each other, so I passed the phone to the African-American man standing nearby who acted as an interpreter between the two of us. He finally made me understand that Dr. Collins was in Oklahoma and that I had to wait at the airport for him to come and get me.

I did not know that Oklahoma was a different state from Texas, where I had landed, and that it was going to take three to four hours for him to come get me. I was stuck at the airport and got a little concerned when he did not show up after some time. However, there was nothing to do except wait, for the guy with the phone was gone and I had no clue why the pay phone kept rejecting my coins. Therefore, there was no need to try calling Dr. Collins again. I was hungry and tired after my twenty-one-hour hour flight, and perplexed, for it was almost 8:00 P.M. and the sun was still shining! What in the world was going on?

Everybody around me seemed to be going about their business without any worry. Maybe there was nothing to be concerned about.

I had arrived in Dallas in the middle of summer and it was strange to me that at that time of day the sun was still up. Remember, I lived in the tropics near the equator all of my life and by 7:00 P.M. there is pitch darkness. I began wondering if God had indeed asked me to come to America. When was Dr. Collins going to come? Why was he taking so long? There was nobody for me to ask these questions or anyone to give me the answers.

Finally, at about 9:00 P.M., Dr. Collins showed up with his son David. I thank God that the gentleman whose phone I used told Dr. Collins which terminal I was in and where he would find me. It was a great relief when he introduced himself, and we got into his car and drove to Waxahachie, for he graciously offered me a place to pass the night.

On our way we stopped to eat dinner at a Cracker Barrel off of Highway 360 in Arlington, Texas. Cracker Barrel Old Country Store Restaurant serves typical home-style American dishes and all of the different food choices were more than confusing. There was no fufu, plantains, cassava, cocoyams, and other foods I was used to eating on the menu, and I had a very hard time ordering anything. Dr. Collins and his son came to my rescue and ordered something for me to eat. Most of what I ate was sweet and did not taste anywhere close to what I grew up eating. I was very hungry and the meal was timely.

This was my first brush with culture shock, and many other instances would occur and leave me in bewilderment and confusion. My cultural intelligence with regard to American food was very low at the time. This brings to mind a true story I heard about some missionaries and their cook. The people the missionaries went to preach to did not know how to read and write the English language, and the missionaries did not know how to adequately convey information in their language. So they instructed their cook to determine the content of canned foods by looking at the picture on the side of the can.

Therefore, each time the cook wanted to prepare, let's say, beans, a can with the picture of beans on its side will be opened. This went on for a while until the missionary couple had a baby and their home church sent them ready-made baby meals. The meals were produced by Gerber and each can had the picture of the head of a baby on its side. The cook was instructed to feed the baby. So the cook picked up one of the cans to open, and was shocked and mesmerized that there was the head of a baby on the can. She screamed, dropped the can, and ran out of the house shouting that the missionary couple was cannibals. They eat babies!

This is a true story even though it may sound absurd, but it is worth noting that outward appearances do not tell the complete story. Therefore, it is unacceptable to judge a book by its cover. This implies that drawing conclusions about people and situations without integrating all available information will lead to faulty conclusions.

I spent the night in Dr. Collins' house in Waxahachie. His wife, Ruth, made sure I was comfortable. I was shown a room upstairs and encouraged to feel at home. She warned me that I could be woken by a loud noise early in the morning, but that I should not be concerned about it. The trains, she went ahead to explain, passed by their house early in the morning and the noise from the train could be a nuisance.

It was getting late and I was ready to catch some sleep and worry about the noise of the train when the time came. A lot had transpired since I left Cameroon and there was little time for me to catch my breath. I fell on my knees and thanked God for bringing me to America, then fell on the bed and was soon overtaken by sleep.

Suddenly, I was jolted out of my deep slumber by a loud noise. I rubbed my eyes and looked at the electronic clock in the room. It was 5:00 A.M. and the train was passing by. I was too tired and sleepy to bother peeping at the train. The noise was not strong enough to keep me awake for long. As the train was still passing by, I fell back into sleep.

"Good morning!" my host called. I dragged myself out of bed, prayed briefly and started my first day in America. Dr. Collins and I hopped into his car and drove from Waxahachie to the University of Texas at Dallas, in

Richardson, Texas. It was a quiet drive. He thought I was coming to the University of Texas at Arlington, in Arlington, Texas, but when he went through my admission letter, he realized I was going to the University of Texas at Dallas, in Richardson, Texas. These university campuses are about 35 miles apart and are separate institutions.

It was very hot that summer, and I was a little surprised by how hot my new country was. We had been driving for quite some time and I had already lost track of where we were when the car started slowing down. We were about to exit from US highway 75, where the legal speed limit is 60 miles per hour, although some cars were going at about 80 miles per hour. I immediately noticed that life here was on the fast lane. Most of my life, the cars I had ridden in were allowed a maximum speed of 40 miles per hour and most of the time cars could not attain such a speed on unpaved, pothole-infested roads. Nothing compared to the excellent roads we were driving on.

We exited and Dr. Collins asked me if I was hungry. Of course, my tummy was already rumbling and some food would do me a lot of good. I started imagining what we were going to eat. Would I be able to order my food? Would the menu be filled with strange choices as it was the previous night? My thoughts were interrupted once more by Dr. Collins. He asked, "Have you had a hamburger before?" I replied, "No." "Then you are going to have your first burger," Dr. Collins said.

The first time I heard about a hamburger was in one of my sociology classes. Our sociology professor said Americanization is preceded by *Coca-colonization* and *McDonaldization*. He went ahead to explain that McDonalds is famous for their hamburgers and they go to great lengths to ensure that no matter where you eat their burger it tastes the same.

Wow! The hamburger must be some sort of gourmet meal, if they have to ensure that it always tastes the same. My mouth was already watering when we pulled in front of a Burger King. We walked to the counter and I saw what looked like bread with some meat sticking out of it. What! Maybe we were in the wrong place, or the gourmet hamburger was not on the displayed menu.

"Eric, what are you going to eat?" Dr. Collins asked. He went on to say something like, "I am having a number 4." I did not know what the different numbers meant, so I said, "I am having a number 4 also, with French fries." The hot, crispy and well-salted French fries, were delicious. And the most anticipated hamburger was nothing close to the gourmet meal I was expecting.

How in the world did I miss it? Well, when you hear things and you think you understand, some of the pictures you paint of them may be very different from the reality. Talking of missing it, a few months later, in the middle of a conversation, somebody asked me if we had houses where I was coming from. Of course we live in houses; I replied. How could this person have missed it?

Back to my hamburger meal, no cutlery was given us to eat with; we just grabbed the burger and munched it, then washed it down with a cold Coke. There was an endless supply of Coke and other non-alcoholic beverages. Hmmm! What a country! I had just had my induction into fast food and how to clean up and dispose of my trash. This was the beginning of all of the learning I had to do to be able to survive in my new country. There were a lot of lessons ahead of me and it would take continuous learning and adjusting on a daily basis to succeed in America.

When God leads us, we cannot just fold our arms and wait for Him to come do those things that are within our power to do. We have to be willing to adjust and change and accommodate growth. We finally got to the University of Texas at Dallas and went to the International Student Office where I was oriented on how to register and rent a house.

After the orientation, we drove back to Waxahachie. On the way we decided that I had to move up to the university the next day, for the commute to and from Waxahachie to the University of Texas at Dallas was a little more than an hour.

All the while, as we were driving, my mind was processing the cost of registering for classes and renting a room and I was devastated. Dr. Collins had been hoping that I was going to be attending UTA, and in one of our e-mails said there was somebody with whom I could share an apartment and that the room would cost about $110. When it turned out that I was going to an entirely different university there was nothing he could do.

We drove back the next day and they dropped me and my single suitcase containing a few clothes at the International Student Office. I was now on my own. I could not move into a house immediately and the Lord used a student from Malawi, East Africa, who was a member of the Association of American Students, to provide a place for me to pass my first night in Richardson, Texas.

I slept on a couch in his living room and was very grateful. The next day this student drove me to school for me to register. I went to the Geosciences Department and asked to see the head of the department. I told him I was a new student from Cameroon and did not have enough money to register. I asked for a teaching assistantship, but was told it was not possible for the department to do anything for me. The head of the department advised me to take classes for at least a semester and my performance would determine if they would consider offering me a teaching assistant position or not. This response did not make my predicament any better or less disheartening.

Now I was faced with tuition costs of slightly more than $4,000 and monthly rent of $260 not including money for books, food, clothing, and health care. All I had on me was slightly more than $2,000. I was stuck. Did God ask me to come to America and go to school at the University of Texas at Dallas? Or was I just here on my own?

So far, the Lord had been faithful and had answered my prayers. I called my wife and told her that things were very tough out here and that if they did not change I was going to come back home. I had obeyed and come to America, and it was left to my Father in heaven to perfect what He had started.

We declared a day of fasting and prayer to humble ourselves before God and ask for his favor and breakthrough. I went ahead and registered for the semester and took a temporal student loan of $4,000 to cover the cost of tuition. I rented a room in a four-bedroom apartment on campus for $260 a month.

Compared to my students days in Cameroon, here I was renting a single room for 182,000 frs CFA when a few years ago I could not rent a room for just 2,000 frs CFA. The change to me was astronomical and only God could perform such a miracle. I had no bed, so I slept on the floor for a few days, until the International Christian Fellowship brought me a bed a few days later. I was very grateful. My faith was strengthened and I knew my Father in heaven was taking care of me and that it was going to be okay.

However, I became homesick and it is difficult to describe how I missed my spouse and son. Those early days were very miserable ones and I was barely having enough to eat. Some mornings, water took the place of milk in my cereal during breakfast.

Despite all of these difficulties I did not feel abandoned or forsaken in any way by my Father in heaven. I remember having a conversation with a roommate from Uganda; he was from a rich family and had saved enough money to come over to the U.S. to do a master's in the School of Management at the University of Texas at Dallas. He could not wrap his mind around the thought of me getting onboard a plane and coming to America without enough money.

I told him God was my sponsor. By the time we separated from that apartment he also could not wrap his mind around some of the things that had happened in my life. He tried to explain it away by saying I was lucky, but I told him I did not believe in luck. God was my source and nothing happened in my life without His knowledge. My Father in heaven is a giver and all things are from Him. For it is written:

What, then, shall we say in response to this? If God is for us, who can be against us? He who did not spare His own Son, but gave Him up for us all—how will He not also, along with Him, graciously give us all things?

—Romans 8:31–32

According to the Scripture above, God has already given us the greatest gift. In fact, He made the provision available before we were aware of our need for a savior. God, in like manner, loves us enough to meet other needs in our lives. It does not matter what the need is, there is nothing too hard for God to do.

As you will discover, things were going to get very tough in the months ahead, but God's grace was also sufficient for me.

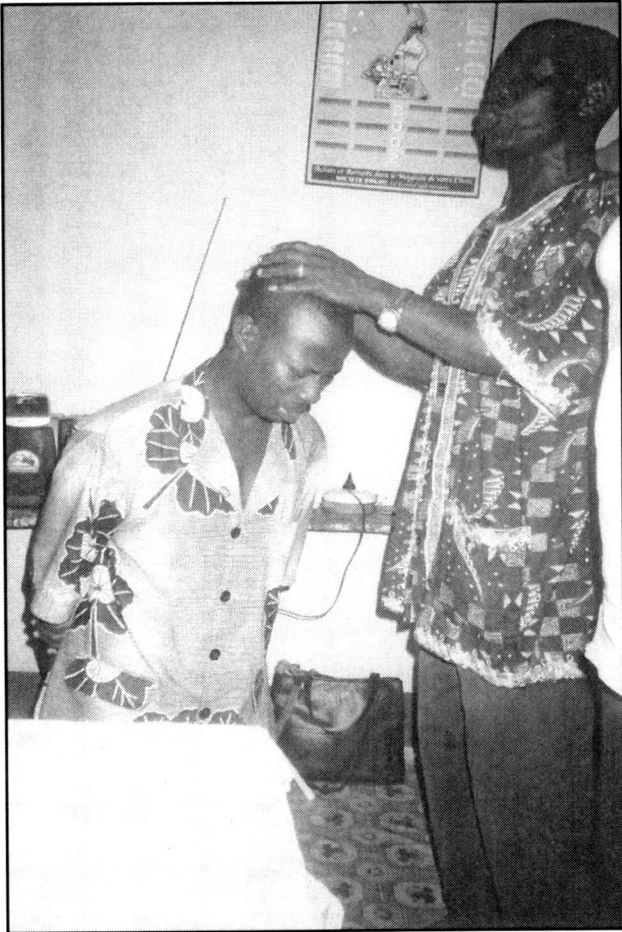

My father praying for me the night I was about to leave Younde to embark on one of the greatest adventures of my life. I was about to leave for the United States of America and my dad was blessing me and praying that my trip would be successful.

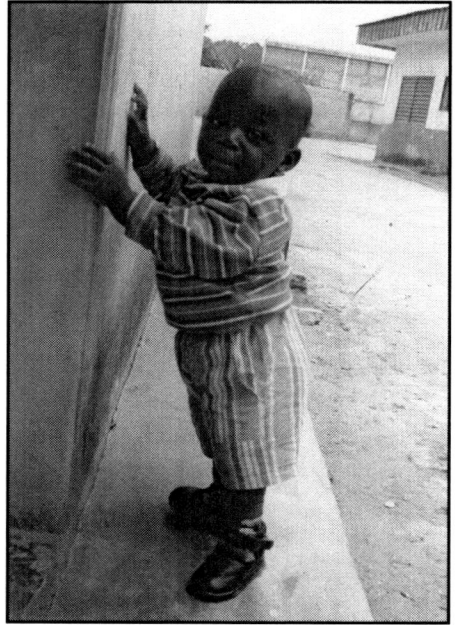

Our son, Afaamboma, shortly before I left for the United States of America. He was about 9 months old here, and is standing with the aid of the wall.

My wife, Elizabeth, with our son Afaamboma, a few months after I had left for the U.S. When I received this picture, it made me more homesick.

CHAPTER 6

AGAINST ALL ODDS

"He replied, 'If you have faith as small as a mustard seed, you can say to this mulberry tree, "Be uprooted and planted in the sea," and it will obey you.'"

—Luke 17:6

I TALKED WITH the secretary of the Geosciences Department at the beginning of the fall semester (my first semester at the University of Texas at Dallas) and was encouraged to apply for a teaching assistant-ship, which I did immediately, and kept talking with the head of the department to do something to alleviate my situation. Classes started during the last week of August 2002 and I settled down to study.

Studies in the United States had peculiar challenges for me. For example, I had very rudimentary knowledge of computers. I did not know what a folder was. And was in total shock and confusion when the teaching assistant asked us in my first remote sensing lab to open a folder and import data into Excel for our lab exercise. We were then instructed to plot the information and export it into Canvas, then write a report in Word and turn it in.

I was completely overwhelmed by the information and got lost during the lab exercise. A thought came into my mind that if studying

63

in the U.S. was going to be this challenging and difficult then I may as well just give up and go try to do something else.

But I reminded myself, first, that my Father in heaven had asked me to come here to study. Second, I encouraged myself not to give up, but face the challenges head on, just as I had done at our bilingual University in Cameroon where I obtained my Masters degree in Earth Sciences.

I arrived at the bilingual university with very little knowledge of French, since I was from the English speaking part of Cameroon. My first graduate-level lecture delivered by a French professor in French was a nightmare. The subject was geology and some of the terminology was similar in English, but it was very difficult to take notes in French. I tried to copy from the students next to me but was hampered since they were writing in shorthand. I felt like a fish that had been taken out of water and was gasping for air.

I immediately decided that I would try to translate what the professor was saying and write it directly in English. Since I was living in a city where French was the dominant language, I was able to learn the language with time and went on to finish the program. This was not the case with some of my English-speaking mates with whom I started the program. Since we had no support system, some of them dropped out of the program.

I did not give up then, so why should I give up now? I pressed on, and most of my classmates were very supportive and helped walk me through some of the computer basics. I was typing with just one finger and had to look at each key before striking it. But as time went on, I caught up with the different computer programs that were needed for my studies and have since improved tremendously.

Computers were just one of my worries. I needed money to pay my tuition and for food. I was homesick and the money I had borrowed was accruing interest at 10% per month. In the midst of all this, I had to do well in the classes I had signed up for, since awarding me a teaching assistantship was going to depend heavily on my performance.

It was during this time that on October 28, 2002, I wrote a letter to a friend. I have edited the letter for grammatical errors and changed a few things, including names to hide the identity of the person. I kept the e-mail because I had the conviction that the Lord was taking care of me and that I was going to need it in the future. I also bring this up to provide firsthand information on the reality of what I was going through. Here is the letter:

Sis,

At the moment I have not been able to get anything going and it is not very easy. I know God is taking care of me, but at times the flesh is weak and impatient. Please continue praying for me that I will wait on the Lord and act according to His will. We borrowed some money for my flight and part of my tuition hoping that when I got here I would get a teaching assistantship, which has not yet happened and last week I received a letter saying that the money is due the second week of December. Three million francs is not a small sum of money back home. I replied that I am not working but God was going to provide the money. He started it and He is going to take it to the expected end. Please continue praying for me. God is doing great things. I was thrilled last week when I prayed for socks and six new pairs of socks were brought to me a few days later. The money for my scholarship has not yet been paid; they are still doing the paperwork, etc. I am more than conquerors through Christ Jesus. The battle is not mine but the Lord's and his name is going to be glorified. I have been through similar things and the Lord has always made a way. He is going to do it again, for He has promised. I do not know how and when but I know God is taking care of me and everything is under His control. We are going to rejoice together when He does it and you will be a witness to what the Lord is doing, that is why I am sharing this with you. Have a good night and extend my greetings to your husband and your entire family.

Your brother in the Lord,

Tangumonkem Eric

Here was the reply:

Bro. Eric,

Have you looked for a job on campus? The University Financial Aid Office will look to see if you are trying to at least work and make some money to repay. American students also have to work to pay their school bills…. they take out loans and some are fortunate enough to have a scholarship or two, but it normally does not pay the entire sum but only helps. Joel is still working and paying off his school bill six years after having graduated. He worked almost the entire time he was schooling as we were unable to pay the whole sum, only a part. He took loans and worked to pay what he could as he studied. It was not easy. Pam is doing the same to finish up her education at this time.

As for the TA-ship, I had one offered to me two years ago at UNT, but it would have only paid for tuition, not for housing and food. I still had to work to pay for housing, food, books, and transportation. TA-ships do not cover everything. Another thing is that when it is only mentioned it is not a conclusion. Everything must be in writing and signed by the officials in power. That is one thing to always remember. Applications have to be made to the proper departments and have signed documents. You cannot make decisions and move without proper documentation, which is what I see has happened. I am sorry that you took the man's word without written confirmation. Now you have to try to find another way until some other means shows up. God can help you, but you must also help yourself by doing your part.

In America we have to work hard for the money we get … it looks as if everyone is prosperous, but the majority is struggling to make ends meet and everyone is working to meet the bills. I hope you understand and don't think that all students are getting scholarships, grants, and everything is paid for them. That is not the norm but rather very unusual.

I am only explaining the reality of how things work in the U.S., I hope you understand so that you don't feel that you are not being treated correctly and are the only one struggling. We all learned to pray hard, work hard, and believe in God to help us when we were in our studies.

This is not meant to discourage or to be angry with you ... please understand that. I am only explaining how things work in this country so that you can better understand how to manage and how to continue on. I wish that you would have consulted us before borrowing money and coming all this way without firm confirmations in writing. Perhaps it would have spared you some struggling ...

Perhaps a TA-ship will come in the future. You need to make a formal application for it. In the meanwhile you also must find work to keep going.

We are praying for you and we care very much. I wish we could help financially but we are not in a position to do that. We can pray and we are doing that.

God encourage and bless you as you serve Him.

In Him,

   Sis.

The response to my letter was a mouthful, and humanly speaking this letter painted an excellent picture of the challenges that were ahead of me. Thank God this friend was very sincere and open. That is what true friends are for; they do not tell you what you want to hear. Instead, they tell you the true state of your situation so that you will know how to move forward.

I was grateful for the letter, because it was a quick reminder that we are always faced with two realities. One involves the physical circumstances surrounding us. That is what we touch, see, taste, hear, and smell with our five senses. It may be sickness, joblessness, depressions, homelessness, poverty, etc. The other is what our Father in heaven says about that particular situation. This involves the faith realm. Our faith is not just wishful thinking. It is knowing, accepting, and believing what God's word says about the situation we are facing. Believing God's word and acting on it is not an easy choice. Our first inclination in most cases is to follow the physical or what we can easily perceive with our five senses.

The question is, "Whose report are we to believe? What reality should we base our decisions on? Which of the 'realities' is real?" I do not refuse the fact that this letter painted the most accurate and vivid picture of the predicament I found myself in. You can also say that I got myself in this predicament. Why did I embark on this journey without adequate funds? What was I thinking? Was it necessary to embark on this journey in the first place? The list of questions could go on and on.

Everything pointed to the fact that I was in for a very tough ride and would need to be strong and courageous. According to the letter, even if I got a teaching assistantship it was not going to be enough to cover my tuition, room, and board. I was between a rock and a hard place. What was I to do?

Praise God that, despite the dire picture that was painted for me, there was another picture that I could reflect upon. This picture was that painted by my Father in heaven. This was the true picture. This was the one and only picture that truly portrayed what I was facing. The reality portrayed by this second picture circumvents that of the picture painted by my friend. But my friend's picture served a very important function.

God's reality is the only true reality and we have to make a conscious decision to walk in God's reality. The reality revealed in God's Word does not refuse or downplay the physical reality that we are facing, but goes beyond the physical and offers hope. God's reality does not only offer hope, it offers a way of escape as stated in the following verse:

> The righteous person may have many troubles, but the LORD delivers him from them all.
>
> —Psalm 34:19

This verse says many troubles, and it does not say God will prevent the troubles from coming into our lives. When the troubles show up, shout for joy, for they are an indication that deliverance is around the corner. Opposites always attract and problems will definitely attract solutions. Do not lose sight; remember for every problem there is a solution. I had many troubles at this point in my life and needed deliverance. My deliverance was not going to come from "my hard physical work" for there was little I could do to change the circumstances surrounding me. My solace was in the promises of my Father in heaven, for it is written:

"Therefore, I tell you, do not worry about your life, what you will eat or drink; or about your body, what you will wear. Is not life more important than food, and the body more important than clothes? Look at the birds of the air; they do not sow or reap or store away in barns, and yet your heavenly Father feeds them. Are you not much more valuable than they? Can any one of you by worrying add a single hour to your life? And why do you worry about clothes? See how the flowers of the field grow. They do not labor or spin. Yet I tell you that not even Solomon in his entire splendor was dressed like one of these. If that is how God clothes the grass of the field, which is here today and tomorrow is thrown into the fire, will He not much more clothe you—you of little faith? So do not worry, saying, 'What shall we eat?' or 'What shall we drink?' or 'What shall we wear?' For the pagans run after all these things, and your Heavenly Father knows that you need them. But seek first his kingdom and his righteousness, and all these things will be given to you as well. Therefore, do not worry about tomorrow, for tomorrow will worry about itself. Each day has enough trouble of its own."
—Matthew 6:25–34

The sure solution to worrying is to focus on what God's word says concerning the circumstances surrounding you. This is the only antidote that will neutralize faithlessness and sustain you through whatever obstacle you are facing. It is the only tried and true way that will unleash the faith necessary to make you an overcomer. You would not be the first person on this road. David was faced with Goliath, a formidable foe. This is how the Bible paints Goliath:

> A champion named Goliath, who was from Gath, came out of the Philistine camp. His height was over six cubits and a span. He had a bronze helmet on his head and wore a coat of scale armor of bronze weighing five thousand shekels; on his legs he wore bronze greaves, and a bronze javelin was slung on his back. His spear shaft was like a weaver's rod, and its iron point weighed six hundred shekels. His shield bearer went ahead of him.
>
> —1 Samuel 17:4–7

As the narrative goes, Goliath had challenged the entire Israelite army every morning for forty days. But nobody was courageous enough to stand up to him. They had many excuses for not doing so. Any excuse for not acting on the reality that transcends all realities is not good enough. God's word concerning whatever obstacle you are facing is the only reality. So let the word of God be your guide and your anchor when faced with insurmountable mountains.

We all won our first race and have the potential to win other races. We are born champions and the only way to remain champions is to operate by the owner's manual. David knew how to use the owner's manual. That is why with little or nothing to show, humanly speaking, he was able to speak and act in a way that experts could not. The Bible paints a very pitiful picture of him:

> Now David was the son of an Ephrathite named Jesse, who was from Bethlehem in Judah. Jesse had eight sons, and in Saul's time he was very old. Jesse's three oldest sons had followed Saul to the war: The firstborn was Eliab; the second, Abinadab; and the third, Shammah. David was the youngest. The three oldest followed Saul, but David went back and forth from Saul to tend his father's sheep at Bethlehem.
>
> —1 Samuel 17:12–15

What was this young shepherd boy thinking? Was he not aware of the danger facing him? What military experience did he have? Why was he trying to show off? What made him think that he could succeed where seasoned experts had failed? David, have you done your homework? Are you sure of what you wanted to get into? The list of questions could go on and on.

What are some of the questions that keep you from seizing the moment and climbing the mountain that is in front of you? Is it your religious traditions? Maybe advice from friends and associates? God's Word never fails, irrespective of how we feel or think. If we dare act on it, we will see the salvation of the Lord. David did just that, for it is written:

> David said to the Philistine, "You come against me with sword and spear and javelin, but I come against you in the name of the LORD Almighty, the God of the armies of Israel, whom you have defied. This day the LORD will hand you over to me, and I'll strike you down and cut off your head. This very day I will give the carcasses of the Philistine army to the birds and the wild animals, and the whole world will know that there is a God in Israel. All those gathered here will know that it is not by sword or spear that the LORD saves; for the battle is the LORD's, and He will give all of you into our hands."
>
> —1 Samuel 17:45–47

David makes us understand that the supernatural always triumphs over the natural. In other words, God's reality is the only reality that counts. Although conventional wisdom states that those with the best weapons will always win the battle, this is not always the case. There is another way to win the battle. You can do it God's way, which is unconventional in many respects. This is my story and how I perceived the challenges that were before me.

That is why in my letter to my friend, dated October 28, 2002, I stated emphatically that, "I am more than conquerors through Christ Jesus. The battle is not mine but the Lord's and His name is going to be glorified. I have been through similar things and the Lord has always made a way. He is going to do it again for He has promised."

"I do not know how and when but I know God is taking care of me and everything is under His control. We are going to rejoice together when He does it and you will be a witness to what the Lord is doing, that is why I am sharing this with you." How could I make such a bold statement in the face of dire circumstances? What made me so sure and confident that things would work out? Just like David, I based my assurance and confidence on God's Word, for Jesus said:

"Heaven and earth will pass away, but my words will never pass away."
—Matthew 24:35

This implies that whatever problems you are facing are temporal and will soon be history. Be it sickness, depression, anxiety, loneliness, hunger, famine, unemployment, etc, they will all pass away. God's word is the only reality that does not change. It is our sure anchor and we have to let it determine our actions. The Word admonishes us to ask and it would be given to us. During this time, I needed some socks and in obedience to God's word, I asked my Father in heaven for some socks. I did not tell anybody that I needed socks. It is amazing how my heavenly Father answered my prayer.

A few days later at about 11:00 P.M., I heard a knock on my door. I got up, opened the door and a Christian brother from Kenya was standing there. He was doing a Ph.D. in Physics. We had met at the International Student Office in August when we had both just arrived and were looking for a place to stay. We got different apartments, and moved in.

I was startled. *What in the world is he doing at my door at this time of the night?* This was sometime in October and our friendship was still at its infancy. When I prayed I was not expecting God to answer my prayer through him. He was a student like me, far from home with many

72

challenges of his own. How could he even think of buying me six pairs of socks? I ushered him in and he handed me a package. I opened it and lo and behold it contained six pairs of brand-new socks.

I was mesmerized and speechless. Six new pairs of socks? Wow! I asked my friend how on earth he knew that I needed socks. He said, "I went to Wal-Mart to buy some items and the Holy Spirit told me to buy socks for you." So he obeyed and bought the socks. I thanked God and thanked him.

You may be wondering why I am making a big deal about six pairs of new socks that cost a few dollars. The issue is not about the socks. It is about the fact that my Father in heaven cares so much about the tiniest details of my life. If He could provide socks, He would also take care of the bigger challenges I was facing. Seeing His involvement in so-called "little things" enabled me to see Him move the "bigger things." For God is not too busy to intervene in "small things," nor intimidated by "bigger things." He is the Lord of all and there is nothing impossible for Him.

We have to win small battles to win big ones. If we believe God for smaller things, our faith will grow and we will be able to believe Him for greater things. Just as David told Saul:

But David said to Saul, "Your servant has been keeping his father's sheep. When a lion or a bear came and carried off a sheep from the flock, I went after it, struck it and rescued the sheep from its mouth. When it turned on me, I seized it by its hair, struck it and killed it. Your servant has killed both the lion and the bear; this uncircumcised Philistine will be like one of them, because he has defied the armies of the living God. The LORD who rescued me from the paw of the lion and the paw of the bear will rescue me from the hand of this Philistine." Saul said to David, "Go, and the LORD be with you."
—1 Samuel 17:34–37

David understood that the heart of the matter is what God can do and that circumstances would change, but God does not change. As the prophet Jeremiah put it:

"Ah, Sovereign LORD, you have made the heavens and the earth by your great power and outstretched arm. Nothing is too hard for you."
—Jeremiah 34:17

God is not limited by the circumstances surrounding us and will see us through if we trust Him. The socks incident taught me that when we pray we should let God answer our prayer when and through whoever He chooses. We become discouraged and give up when we fix our eyes on some particular mechanism or means through which we expect our prayers to be answered.

I was very thankful and encouraged that the Lord was at work and that He was going to see me through. My struggles were far from over and the first order of business was to pay my tuition.

I had arrived in the U.S. with a little more than $2,000 and my tuition was more than $4,000. I applied for a temporary student loan to pay for my tuition. I say the loan was temporary because I was expected to pay the loan in its entirety by the end of the semester. This meant I was left with virtually no money to buy food. Remember, I had mentioned that my mother had travelled to Maryland for a visit. She flew down to Dallas to see me before leaving for Cameroon and gave me $500. Thank God for mothers who are always caring and sharing.

CHAPTER 7

CONVERSATIONS WITH GOD

"Ask and it will be given to you; seek and you will find;
knock and the door will be opened to you."
—Matthew 7:7

BEING AN INTERNATIONAL student meant I was not allowed to work off campus. The only place I was allowed to work was on the university campus. Some of the potential jobs were handing out tickets for parking violations, serving food in the student cafeteria, manning the front desk at the student gymnasium, being an office assistant, etc. The jobs were few and highly sought-after by all of the international students. I tried hard to get an on-campus job, but to no avail. This meant that there was no way for me to pay the loan that I had taken.

We kept praying and I kept asking the Geosciences Department to do something about my situation. At last the Lord answered our prayer and I was awarded a scholarship worth $1,000 by the Geosciences Department. This was the beginning of my breakthrough. I was very happy and grateful.

Although the scholarship was only $1,000, it was worth more in that it immediately qualified me for in-state tuition, which at that

75

time was slightly more than $2,000. This meant that my international student tuition of more than $4,000 dropped by 50%. All of a sudden my temporary loan was completely accounted for. What a relief this brought to me and my family.

I could now focus on my studies and make good grades. Then the department head and the graduate adviser by the end of the semester would see if there was a possibility of offering me a teaching assistantship.

Textbooks were also expensive; for example, $120 was the price of the textbook for my remote sensing class. Therefore I borrowed textbooks from other colleagues who had taken the courses before me. This help was God-sent to me and I will be forever grateful for all of the help I received from these course mates. The semester progressed slowly and things did not get better.

Yes, my tuition had been covered, but the money I borrowed in Cameroon was accruing at the rate of 10% a month. I was not making any money and there was no way for me to start making payments on the loan. There was no way to renegotiate with my creditors for they insisted that the original terms of the loan had to be respected. The reason being that I was in America and should do all I could to ensure that I repaid the loan in its entirety.

How was I ever going to pay this huge sum of money? When was I going to pay back the loan? Another question that plagued me at this time was how and when my spouse and son would be able to join me in the U.S. There were no easy answers; all I could do was to trust the Lord. There was nothing within my power that I could do to change the situation. I just had to work hard in school and wait for the Lord to do something concerning my situation.

During this time of waiting I wrote down some prayers:

November 20, 2002: Faith is being sure of what we hope for and certain of what we do not see, because God who has promised and who is the object of our faith is faithful and worthy to be trusted. Father, you are the owner of all the silver, gold, diamonds, dollars, etc., and all the resources on earth and in the entire universe. You do not encourage laziness, but the law of this land does not permit me to work. We owe more than three million francs, my wife and son have to come here, and my tuition and fees have to be paid. The amount seems so great to me and I cannot imagine how it is going to come. After all it is impossible with Eric for I see very little and my feelings are saying how is it going to work, etc.? Lord, it is going to work because impossibilities are possible with you and I stand aside and watch what you are doing and all the glory be given to you. I will testify of the goodness of our God and some people will say, "Oh! It was easy," but with Eric it is not possible; it is possible with God. Thank you, Jesus, for this opportunity to see your hand. To you be the glory. In Jesus' name I pray, amen.

Five days later, I wrote down yet another prayer:

November 25, 2002: Since the other day, I have been troubled in my soul because it seems things are not moving, humanly speaking. Father, I know you are God and you reign over all creation. You created me for a purpose and brought me here for signs and wonders. Thank you for all of the uncertainties and all of the obstacles. The bigger the mountain the bigger the miracle. Lord you started it and will complete it. I am going to cry again. I am not ashamed to cry, for I am free to express myself before the Lord. Lord, I will not go to Egypt for help. Sustain me and have your way in my life. Thank you, Lord, for giving me the opportunity for my faith to be tried and for it to be exercised and grow stronger. In Jesus' name I pray, amen.

I wrote down another prayer three days later:

November 28, 2002. Lord Jesus, thank you for bringing me to this country. There are a lot of distractions and it seems very foolish to depend and trust you, and more attractive to go the way of the masses. Even as Daniel, Lord, I have resolved not to defile myself. Not by power, not by might, but by your spirit. Lord I strongly desire this and let me stand for the truth, no matter the cost. Let me go the extra mile for the glory of your name. In Jesus' name I pray, amen.

The next day, I wrote down this prayer,

November 29, 2002. The law of the land says I should not work and your Word says if I do not work, I should not eat. Lord, make a way out for me to work. It is impossible in my eyes, but Lord, make a way for me to earn some money that will take care of my needs and my wife and son and family. I have come to the end of myself and do not know what to do. Lord Jesus, give me the grace to stand for you and do what you want me to do, to take the right move. In Jesus' name I pray, amen.

During this difficult period, I had to come clean before my Father in heaven and tell him exactly how I was feeling and some of the crazy thoughts that were running through my mind. I realized that He already knew them and it would do me much good if I just went ahead and told Him anyway.

The story of the man with a son who had an evil spirit came to my mind. This man brought his sick son to the apostles, but they had a hard time trying to drive out the evil spirit that was tormenting his son. Jesus had to come to their aid:

> Jesus asked the boy's father, "How long has he been like this?" "From childhood," he answered. "It has often thrown him into fire or water to kill him. But if you can do anything, take pity on us and help us." "If you can?" said Jesus. "Everything is possible for him who believes." Immediately the boy's father exclaimed, "I do believe; help me overcome my unbelief!"
>
> —Mark 9:21–24

The boy's father was not ashamed to tell Jesus that he had issues with unbelief. The good news is that Jesus answered his prayer and healed his son. You have to tell the Lord where you are and how you are. The truth of the matter is that He knows all about you and what you are going through.

Let me shed some light on some of the issues raised in the prayers. First of all, I told my Father in heaven that He was the one owing the money I borrowed and was going to pay the debt that I had incurred to come to the U.S. This was a dramatic shift on my part and the burden was uplifted from me and placed on God.

I made this paradigm shift because one evening when I came back from school and was doing the dishes, I remember standing at the kitchen sink and having this conversation in my mind. I strongly believe that the enemy of my soul was trying to mock me and make me doubt God.

It went on like this: "If God is God why did He let you get into debt? Why did God not throw down a big bag of money from heaven with all the money I needed to travel to the U.S.? Doesn't the Bible say God is the provider? Why did He let me get into debt?"

The voice went on to say, "You are on your own and in big trouble." I immediately spoke back in my mind and said, "Lord do you hear what the Enemy is saying? You let me get into debt. No. No. You could have provided some other way. It was your idea for me to embark on this journey in the first place."

"Since you decided to provide through a loan, Lord, you are the one owing the money and will have to pay off the money that you enabled me to borrow." Immediately, I was relieved in my spirit and the Lord would answer this prayer within a few months.

CHAPTER 8

LET GO OF THE U.S.

"Why not say—as some slanderously claim that we say—Let us
do evil that good may result? Their condemnation is just!"
—Romans 3:8

I WAS STILL hard-pressed financially since I could not make any money legally, and the options I had before me to make money were to declare political asylum, get married to somebody, or quit school and work illegally. I could not use any of these options.

First, I left Cameroon on my own volition; therefore, lying that I was chased out of the country was not an option. Second, I was already married and there were no grounds on which to divorce my spouse and remarry. Third, God had asked me to come to the U.S. and go to school, and to school I had to go. So I called my spouse, who at this time was going through her own challenges that are the subject of another book, and told her that if the bottom fell out I would come back to Cameroon and not remain in the U.S. and engage in activities that would not glorify the Lord.

Literally, I had to mentally and emotionally give up my dream of living in the United States of America. Since I was willing to let go of the U.S., the pressure to compromise became weaker. In most cases, compromise is a result of fear, the fear of losing what you hold so dear can drive you to do all in your power to preserve it. But we are not supposed to operate in fear. This can be done by focusing on the Giver instead of the gift.

When this is done, you will realize that you can do without most of what the Enemy is telling you is crucial for your survival. When you focus on your needs and not on the Provider you will make wrong choices. Remember, after Jesus had fasted for forty days, He became hungry, but chose to focus on God's word and not on His hunger:

> Then Jesus was led by the Spirit into the desert to be tempted by the devil. After fasting forty days and forty nights, he was hungry. The tempter came to him and said, "If you are the Son of God, tell these stones to become bread." Jesus answered, "It is written: Man shall not live on bread alone, but on every word that comes from the mouth of God."
>
> —Matthew 4:1–4

I was made to understand that America was not the only place that God would prosper me in. That it is more profitable for me to obey God's word than disobey His word, and live in the U.S. at all cost. In the first place, coming to America was not completely dependent on me. God was the Initiator and the Prompter and He was more than able to finish what He had started. I was also encouraged by the story of how Daniel and the other Jewish boys conducted themselves while they were in captivity in Babylon. The king had instructed them to be fed with the best wine and foods of the land:

> But Daniel resolved not to defile himself with the royal food and wine, and he asked the chief official for permission not to defile himself this way … At the end of the ten days they looked healthier and better nourished than any of the young men who ate the royal food. So the

guard took away their choice food and the wine they were to drink and gave them vegetables instead.

—Daniel 1:8, 15–16

So what is the deal with you, Daniel? You are in captivity and the king has asked you to eat. Why do you want to disobey the orders of the king? Do you not know that you are endangering your life? It is *just* food, Daniel, *just* eat and it will be well with you. Have you not heard that *God helps those who help themselves?* What good will eating only vegetables do to you?

Daniel knew one thing: God's law is to be obeyed above any other law. He and the three other Hebrew boys understood that it is better to please the Lord than please man. It is better to follow what God's word teaches than follow the dictates of our fears. In my case, the fear was; not making it in America and being repatriated to Cameroon. What are you afraid of?

I was facing a lot of challenges because I did not have proper documentation to earn money in the U.S. People started suggesting possible ways for me to solve my problems. No problem is ever yours. God has promised to be with us all the time and we have to take Him at His word.

One suggestion was for me to declare political asylum. I was told most people do it and that it was a sure way for me to get legal papers to work. I was shocked. I told this individual that I had left my country on my own will and did not know why I had to lie that I was a political victim.

I understand that the economic situation in Cameroon is degrading, but that is not a good reason for me to say that I was running away from political persecution in my country, although I had been rough-handled by security forces at a point in my life and I still carry scars on my body. This incident had nothing to do with politics *per se*, and I had no grounds to seek political asylum.

This is not an attempt to downplay the fact that I almost lost my life in the hands of a brutal security officer who had no regard for the law and the dignity of a fellow countryman. What happened to me is not unique in any way. I was just a victim like many other victims in my country who are exploited, abused, and tortured by those who are supposed to protect and defend them.

Maybe I was in the wrong place and with the wrong people as the commanding officer made me understand. But the events that took me to where the law enforcement officer brutalized me were beyond my control. I was struggling to make a living in a country where thousands of young men and women who graduate each year with bachelor's degrees have little prospect of any meaningful employment.

After graduating with a bachelor's degree in geology, there wasn't much I could do to earn a living. I immediately went into action with whatever resources I had. After all, education is to open the mind and empower us to take advantage of our environment. Both formal and informal education equips us with the proper tools to be productive citizens and add value to others.

Here I was with a bachelor's degree, but was about to start making a living with my informal education. When I was six, my mum gave me my first ware to take out and sell. This was "*puff puff*," a type of dough made with wheat flour and deep fried. I had to carry this from one end of the village to the other, usually early in the morning before school time. As I went around the village, I had to shout at the top of my voice, "fine puff puff;" this was done to notify others about my goods. This caught their attention and they would call me and buy what I was selling. It helped a lot and I was able to sell "puff puff" all the time I went out.

Each time before going out, the "puff puff" was counted and I had to make sure I came back with equivalent cash. I had to pay attention, because there were always older boys who wanted to trick me and take my "puff puff" without paying. I also had to overcome shame and develop a love for interacting with different people. Many kids felt uncomfortable doing what I was doing and at times some people would ask me sarcastically why I was having only "fine puff puff" and not "bad puff puff."

As I grew older, I also moved around with my parents to different markets to sell clothes and other goods. Everywhere we lived, we would sell something and that became an integral part of our lives. We did a lot of bargaining then and I had a sense of satisfaction from buying something, selling it to some other person, and making a profit in the process.

This explains why, after graduation, I decided to buy and sell assorted fruits, dried shrimp, and fish. I had no capital to start the business, but Uncle Alfred, my mother's younger brother, gave me 20,000 frs CFA ($35). He sacrificed to provide this much need—seed capital for me to start doing something. I used the money to buy some green bananas and kept them until they got ripe so that I could sell them.

I had heard from other merchants that the fishing communities that lived on small islands off the coast of Cameroon did not grow any food, but caught a lot of fish and shrimp. Therefore, they depended on the mainland for most of their food supply. Meanwhile, the mainland depended on them for fish, shrimp, and other sea foods. Middlemen were needed to make this exchange feasible. That's how I got involved in buying assorted vegetables, fruits, bananas, and plantains to sell on these islands and on my way back I would buy dried fish and shrimp to sell on the mainland. The capital I had was very small. In fact, it could buy me just 40 average meals, but I had to start believing that the money was going to grow.

It was a daring move on my part since I had no contacts on these islands and there wasn't any guarantee that the dried fish and shrimp brought to the mainland would be sold. Entering any new market is always a challenge; it is difficult to penetrate and gain market share when other vendors are fully established.

As such, my first trip was filled with a lot of anxiety, but I prayed and got onboard a canoe with fruits and vegetables that my fiancée had purchased for me without knowing what was ahead of me. On my way,

I spoke with the other vendors who were going to sell similar items and some of them were kind enough to tell me what to do when we landed on the islands.

For example, to keep the vegetables fresh, I was instructed to sprinkle some water on them and place them on the roofs of the shacks in which we were going to sleep, so that the cool night breeze would prevent them from withering. I was also instructed that I had to carry the vegetables in a large container and crisscross the island so that the Islanders could see my wares and buy them.

Early the next morning, I got up and carried the vegetables and heard people calling out to me "njama njama" boy. What they meant was, "Vegetable boy, come and sell us your vegetables." It was one thing to carry things on my head and sell them when I was a kid, and a whole new dimension as an adult to be seen hawking vegetables on an island and being called a boy by people who in some instances were younger than me. Maybe I was too young in their eyes, or they had been accustomed to calling all who sell to them "boys."

Well, this did not prevent me from doing what I went there to do. That is, sell my food stuff, buy dried fish and shrimp, and bring them back to the mainland to sell. It was a little difficult convincing the islanders to buy my fruits and vegetables at a price that would enable me to make a profit. Fortunately, bargaining was something that I had done several times and I knew how much we had paid for what I was trying to sell to them. There was no way I was going to sell for anything below what I paid for. I had to factor in the cost of paying people to load my wares in the boat, offloading when we landed, and my transport fare.

The system was set up in such a way that you were not allowed to put in your goods or take them out of the boat even if you wanted to. This was done so that the "beach boys" on the mainland and the islands could make a cut on the trade. You can imagine my resentment of these guys who were doing all in their power to cut into the little profit I was trying to make. I was not against them making a living, but was barely having enough money to keep my business afloat. My wares were small enough for me to load and offload from the canoe by myself without help.

Some merchants who had more money, had huge loads that definitely needed other people to help them move, and the services of the "beach boys" came in handy. I did not need their services, but there was nothing I could do about it. I would soon discover that many other things would pop up that I could do nothing about.

Selling the fruits and vegetable was easy compared to buying the dried fish and shrimp. The price of shrimp both on the mainland and islands was very volatile. The shrimp had no fixed price and you bought it by using your eyes and also weighing the shrimp by hand. This was done by carrying the large plastic bags in which the dried shrimp were stored, estimating the weight, and offering a price.

Those who had done this over the years had honed their skills to the point where lifting a plastic bag of shrimp gave them an idea of how much it would cost, and how much to sell it for when they went to the mainland. This was not a skill that could be easily transferred and I had to learn fast and on my own. I finally summoned the courage and bought a few bags of shrimp during my first trip back to the mainland.

When I got to the market on the mainland, I realized that the vendors there would not be particularly happy if I tried to retail my shrimp, so I gave it out to them to retail and then had them pay me at the end of the day. I waited for them to sell the shrimp and pay me the amount we had agreed upon. It took some networking and intense negotiations for some of the vendors to take my shrimps.

On the average it took me about five days to go to the islands, sell, buy and come back to the mainland. The journey was usually done in a small canoe propelled by a small fifteen-horsepower Yamaha engine. Wooden canoes are notorious for leaking in water. As such, somebody had to constantly bail out the ever-present pool of water at the bottom of the canoe. The journey on many occasions was without any dramatic events, but on some days the rain would fall on us because the canoe had no roof, and on another occasion the engine broke down when we were still in the creeks leading to the open sea.

The boat owner threw down the anchor and we just passed the night in the boat. The mosquitoes fed on our blood all night. The next morning, the engine was repaired and we completed our journey.

The scariest day of my travels on the sea was when we headed into a storm and the waves pounded and rocked our little canoe to an extent that we thought the canoe was going to capsize. We kept riding one large wave after another, and when the canoe got to the crest of the wave it would barely stay at the top and then rapidly drop to the trough of the wave. This went on and on for what seemed an eternity and we feared for our lives.

The usually calm and pristine waters were suddenly violent and dark, and to make matters worse the rain started pouring heavily. We were in the midst of a storm and the only way was the way forward. Our small fifteen-horsepower engine was no match for the waves and it kept going out on us. At one point the canoe would be headed towards the shore and the waves would jolt the canoe and it would make a U-turn and start going in the opposite direction.

This scared us and we had every reason to be afraid, since none of us had a life jacket. Life jackets were expensive and we just went without them. Everything has an end, even a stormy ocean. With time the rain subsided and the waters calmed enough for us to sail to dry land. This is the closest I got to wishing I was doing something else. Apart from the bedbugs and filthy beds that one slept on and the unsanitary conditions on the islands, the islanders were generally friendly and we were not bothered.

The majority of the people who lived on the islands were from Nigeria and they did not have a residence permit. By law, they were expected to pay a certain sum of money each year to get a resident permit. Most of these fishermen did not pay the fee. As such, once in a while the forces of law and order would storm the islands to enforce the law. Everybody found on the islands was expected to show their national identity card. It is common practice on the mainland for the police officers to stop any vehicle at any time and ask all the passengers to show their identification papers. If it turns out that you do not have a national identity card on you, you were forced to "settle them"; that is you just give them a bribe and they would let you go.

If they found out you were a foreigner without your residence permit, the bribe would be much larger. The accents of the foreigners easily gave them away and it was not difficult for the policemen and gendarmes to identify who was a Cameroonian and who was not. The gendarmes in particular are notorious for their brutality and are greatly feared by foreigners.

It was during one of my business trips that I had a brutal reality check with the gendarmes. We had just alighted from our canoe when the orders were issued by a gendarme banishing a rifle that we should all stand in a straight line. I was positioned somewhere in the middle of the line and knew that being a Cameroonian national there was nothing for me to worry about.

This would not be the case, however, as I was soon to discover. The gendarme approached me and asked for my national identity card. I handed him my university ID card, and he took the card from me and told me that this was not an identification document. He then moved to the next person in front of me. I turned slightly and was whispering with the other person who was behind me that I do not know why my school ID was not sufficient to identify me. It had my picture and I had just graduated.

I was naïve enough to think the gendarme officer would recognize the university, for it was the only state university in the province where we were. At that moment, there were six state universities in the country, and they were fairly well known. Back then the national identification cards issued in Cameroon were paper and easily got damaged by the rain and high humidity associated with maritime travel. In contrast to a paper national identification card, my university ID card was laminated and insulated, which prevented it from being destroyed by the rain and high humidity. I thought traveling with a robust university card was a wise move on my part.

The gendarme officer did not think so. Without warning, I felt a heavy blow on my left shoulder and I came crashing down on the wet sand on the beach. Everything happened so fast that I had to piece together the sequence of events when I got up and sat on my buttocks. The gendarme officer had pounded my shoulder with the butt of his rifle and kicked both of my legs at the same time. This caused me to lose my balance and subsequently fall on the sand.

When I got up and sat on my buttocks, he instructed me not to move or get up, for if I did he was going to shoot me. He said, "I will shoot you and only the president can ask me why." What in the world had I done that deserved death? Why was this fellow being so mean? What was I to do next?

All of these questions were still running through my mind when I felt something warm on my chest. I was bleeding and did not even realize it. The events had put me in a state of shock and blood was oozing from a wound torn on my left shoulder by the butt of the gun. I was not aware of the damage that had been done to my shoulder until I started feeling the blood running down my chest.

The canoe owner rushed to the commanding officer and reported the incident to him. The commandant dispatched another gendarme officer to come and get us. The gendarme who assaulted me refused to leave. He only left after a second officer was sent. When we got in front of the commandant he asked me to tell him what had happened. By this time a large crowd had gathered in the hall where the commandant was sitting.

After I finished my explanation, the commandant turned and addressed the crowd, saying that we university students were rude and mean to our professors. He went on to say that if I thought I was better than them, I would not be in the middle of the ocean scraping for a living. The commandant made me to understand that he had a first school living certificate (6th grade) and was now a commandant, but I was in a pathetic situation because I had nothing to show for the many years spent in school. He added, "By the way, if you think you are smart because you have a bachelor's degree, I am sponsoring my younger brother who is studying for a doctorate degree."

Up to this point, despite the severe injury and the pain from the wound I had sustained, I had not shed a tear. But the words of this commandant, who is supposed to know better, broke my heart and I wept. I was not weeping because my wound was hurting, though it was. I was weeping for a country that could care less about its youths. A country where the leaders pay lip service to the promise of giving the young people a chance, but have no willingness to keep their promise. I grew up hearing that youths are the leaders of tomorrow.

As with many other slogans used by politicians, this one was a toothless bulldog. When are the youths going to lead when the same person has been president for over twenty-five years? Is it that the current president is the best individual the country has ever produced? I doubt it. When leaders use the strong arm of the law to intimidate, harass, and brutalize their own people, they are nothing but selfish, self-serving, and self-centered tyrannical dictators. We can complain all we want of "brain drain" to the West, but it will not amount to anything if our leaders do not care about the dignity of other people. Cameroon belongs to all its citizens and some are not more equal than others. Those in power must recognize that they were elected to serve the people and not the other way around.

After giving his speech, the commandant asked me to go. That was it. I had to go treat myself at my own expense. Here was a young Cameroonian who had just finished school and was trying to create a job and earn a living instead of staying at home and waiting for handouts from his family, but he was not receiving any encouragement from the authorities. Those who were supposed to protect him were harassing and brutalizing him.

There was nothing I could do to my abusers, than to move on with my life. But I can appreciate what others have suffered in the hands of unscrupulous law enforcement officers. This abuse and torture will continue unless the people stand up and demand that their rights be respected. It is not an easy proposition, for, when people believe that breaking the law for momentary gain is the only way forward, the *status quo* will remain.

I discovered that to survive in my business and to make a profit, I had to make some difficult choices. The taxes we were required to pay were way too many. Why was nobody doing something about it? Why was there no talk of tax reform? The answer is that most people preferred to break the law rather than fix it. We were required to pay a tax when we bought the fish, pay one when we landed at the beach on the mainland, and pay another tax when we went to the market to sell the dried fish and shrimp. All of these taxes were in addition to the other fees that one had to pay for loading and offloading the goods.

For beginners like me whose capital was very small, the taxes and fees put us under a lot of stress and threatened to cripple our businesses. Therefore, many people opted to give the tax collector about 50 percent of what they were required to pay. The tax collector did not issue a receipt, but put the money in his personal coffers.

I insisted on paying the taxes in full and getting my receipts. I did this for some time and realized that I was left with very little. This prompted me to take positive action to ensure that the tax code was revised. On one particular day we landed on the mainland beach and the tax collector came to collect his taxes. However, I said we were not going to pay a dime. Prior to our docking, I had mobilized the other people who were in the boat with me and we had arranged to stick to the plan not to pay a thing.

We stood our ground and the guy collecting the taxes threatened to seize our goods. I told him to go ahead and do that. He went to council and brought reinforcement and a tractor, and all of our goods were seized. Things were happening very rapidly and taking a dimension I had not anticipated. All of us boarded the tractor and it took us to the city council, where I requested to see the mayor. Unfortunately, the mayor was not on site and there was nothing the other councilors could do.

I enquired why we had to pay multiple taxes and they told me that in the past the islanders brought the seafood and sold it on the mainland. With time, merchants from the mainland decided to go and buy goods directly from the islanders, so the merchants were then required to pay the tax the islanders paid in the past when they brought their goods to the mainland. As to why we had to pay when we bought on the island, they said it was none of their business. They also were not willing to address the fact that when we paid the landing tax and took our goods to the market we were required to pay another tax.

There wasn't much we could do, but I explained to them that the tax code was outdated and that provision should be made for young graduates who were trying to make a living with very little capital. The spokesperson for the council thought I was diving into issues that were out of my jurisdiction. I made him to understand that I was not against people paying taxes, but when you over-tax it discourages investment and small business will not survive. The approach of one size fits all does more harm than good.

In a country where youth unemployment is about 70%, the last thing you want to do is discourage those who are entrepreneurial and are courageous enough to venture out on their own to create jobs. The authorities did not seem to care and nothing was done to reduce our tax burden. We paid what the council wanted us to pay, and they gave us back our goods and we left.

When I got to the market the next day, the tax lady showed up and I said I wasn't going to pay any tax. I showed her all the receipts of all the other taxes already paid and she said I was in a different council and that area needed tax revenue. My goods were seized again. This time, we were in the market and I decided to beckon for sympathy from the crowd that had gathered. I raised my voice and spoke loud enough for everybody to hear me while I made the point that taxes are good, but they should be applied with consideration. They did not expect me to go sit at home and depend on my parents for my daily needs after all they have been through trying to secure a good education for me.

Most of the people identified with my predicament, for they too had children who upon graduation with a bachelor's or a master's degree were at home with nothing to do and still depending on their parents to feed and clothe them. Most of these graduates were waiting for white collar jobs that were as scarce as dog tears. The majority felt venturing to do anything that would get their hands dirty would reduce their dignity. Who could blame them? Many people would not survive the hostile socio-economic environment that permeates the country.

My pleas yielded some fruit and I did not pay a tax that day, or any other time after that until the day I folded my business and went to graduate school. The lady collecting the tax simply left me alone. I wish the whole system would be re-engineered and adjusted so that young people could be given a chance. There wasn't enough time for me to do anything about the situation.

Through all of this, I learned that there is dignity in labor, and that the job title is not more important than the fact that your job is enabling you to pursue your dreams. I could identify with the challenges faced by the youths. My resolve to stand for what is right and to uphold the law was strengthened.

That is why, when people were advising me to falsify documents and declare political asylum, I refused. It was a tough decision and those around me did not make it any easier. All I heard was gloom and doom. I remember having a phone conversation with somebody who told me that my life in the U.S. was going to be very difficult if I did not get papers (green card) as soon as possible. This individual said, "Who do you think you are? What makes you think you are different? I know of pastors who have followed the asylum route to get papers. By the time you declare political asylum to get papers you will be in great distress."

I calmly replied that I was not going to help God and solve my problem the way other people were solving theirs. I understood that I was going to have a difficult time, so let it be. I would rather obey God than try to pretend that I was the person in charge of my life. My stance did not make any sense to most of my friends. Here I was, without money and in big debt with a possible solution to my predicament, but I was not willing to use it. I appeared foolish in many quarters for suggesting that only those who truly deserve political asylum should apply for it.

Most of these individuals did not know that it had taken many years for this conviction to take hold of me. This takes me back to my second year at the University of Buea in Cameroon. I usually had conversations with my friends about corruption in Cameroon and the benefits of maintaining integrity at all cost.

I was of the opinion that our societal ills were rooted in the fact that many people were not willing to stand up for what is right. Many people preferred "taking advantage of the system." It was easy to bribe and cheat and break the laws of the country as long as this enabled you get what you wanted.

Many people asked, "What harm is being done when you are just trying to survive and take care of yourself? What is wrong in taking advantage of the system? As long as you do not harm anybody in the process and are not caught for breaking the law it is okay."

We would argue back and forth and I would say there was no need to take advantage of the system. We had to obey the law, since breaking the law would set a bad precedence for others. If everybody broke one part of the law, we would end up with a broken system.

I was naïve, as many of them tried to make me understand. They were right on one point: talk is cheap. A time of testing was coming to me. Was I ready to pass the test? Could I stand up for my convictions? How prepared was I to live by what I had been telling others to abide by? Could I take the heat?

I would soon find out that it is not easy to walk on the narrow road. I have stumbled many times and I will possibly stumble again. But in this particular situation I was able to bounce back. I found myself in a very precarious situation during continuous assessment in my second year at the University of Buea. I found myself between a rock and a hard place and the pressure was too much so I caved in big time. I was unable to follow my convictions and all my talk of maintaining integrity and abiding by the law evaporated in the heat of the moment.

It was a regular practice of mine to set up goals at the beginning of each semester, pray for these goals and pursue them during the course of the semester. At the beginning of this particular semester, I had prayed that I would make A grades in two particular geology courses. This was quite a lofty desire, for an A grade was very difficult to come by. In most cases, something like 10% of a class of 48 students got A's. In fact, A grades were so scarce that even desiring to earn an A grade was almost asking for too much.

The continuous assessment was 30% of the final grade. We were taking continuous assessments for two of the courses I had desired to earn A grades in, and I did not know what to write. I had not prepared for the test because we had a field trip, but it seems the other students were ready for the test. I was in a very difficult situation for I was completely blank. What was I to do? Do nothing and get a zero? Write and still not get a passing grade? What would become of the A grades I desired to have? I wanted the A's very badly, for this was going to improve my GPA. I immediately realized that if I failed the continuous assessment, it would be impossible to get A grades and my GPA would not improve.

I was hard pressed to do something. I was not a bad student, but this particular situation was now beyond my control. I had to write something, so I asked a friend who was sitting by me to share his answers with me. This friend willingly allowed me to copy his solutions. I was down to the third question when it suddenly occurred to me that I was cheating in an exam. This was in complete violation of all that I had been telling my friends. What would I tell them after this test, especially the friend from whom I was copying?

I had to choose between making A's in the two courses and standing by my convictions. What was the way forward? I did something that I had never done before. It was a crazy act for me and it took all of the courage and determination I had to choose the latter. I was already

96

cheating and since I had nothing to write, I shredded my answer sheet and walked out of the exam room. What on earth was I doing? It was one of the most difficult things I had ever done.

At the same time, I was fighting an inner battle in my mind. How could I let go of the A grades? I did not have an excuse to give for not taking the continuous assessment. I had already lost 30% of the grade and had just kissed my two would-be A grades goodbye. The professor had instructed us that there would be no make-ups. I was toast. It was very unsettling, but I felt I had to do what I did.

It was not an easy decision. I felt foolish and irrational walking out of the class. In fact, walking the few feet from where I was sitting to the door felt like walking across a soccer pitch. It was as if all the eyes of the other students were piercing at me as I walked out. But the reality is that the students were focused on taking their test and not on me and my lack of preparation.

After what seemed like ages, I made it to the door and into the corridor. Then it finally hit me that I had walked out of an examination room without writing anything for the very first time since starting my academic career. I had horrible feelings of defeat and shame, but deep in me I knew that I had made the right decision. I would rather fail the class than compromise what I stood for.

The papers of the test were graded and my friend from whom I had copied the solutions did not do well. A great portion of the class also did not do well. As a result, the professor changed his mind and declared that those who had missed the assessment and those who took and failed the assessment would be given a second chance to retake the continuous assessment.

Boy oh boy! I was overjoyed for a second chance. I studied hard, went and took the test, and made an A grade on the continuous assessment. I also made A's on the finals. My final grades for the two courses were A's.

This particular semester tested my faith in another area. I was not very good in French and by the grace of God had passed French 101. I was left with French 102. Things were not going very well and I was afraid that I would not pass. My concerns were exacerbated by the fact that some students, after passing all courses in their majors, would not be awarded their degrees at the end of the program because they could not pass French. I have friends who finally gave up and have never gotten their bachelor's degree.

With such apprehension, I went in to take my French 102 exam and got stuck on some of the questions. Suddenly, I heard whispering from a student standing by me. Apparently this student was done with the exam and was on her way to hand in the answers, when it seems she realized I was stuck and stopped to help me. I did not know the student and as soon as she pointed out what I had to do, I filled in the blank spaces feverishly. Was she God sent? How on earth did this perfect stranger know that I was stuck? What made her want to break the law and help me?

My relief was turned into sudden anguish when the course instructor cleared his throat loudly to the hearing of the entire class. This was done to draw our attention and to let us know that he was aware of what was going on by my desk.

This was a rude awakening for me. I had been caught red-handed cheating in an exam. My heart raced and sweat began to pour onto my brow. What was the best thing to do? How was I ever going to get out of this situation?

Penalties for cheating in exams were stiff. But this was nothing compared to the shame and embarrassment that I felt. How on earth did I allow the fear of failure to overwhelm me? Where was my tough talk of integrity and moral uprightness? It seems all had evaporated in the face of difficulties.

All was not lost. I immediately erased what the other student had shown me before the course instructor arrived at my desk. When he got there, I came clean and explained to him what had happened. The instructor waited for me to finish my explanation and after what seem like an eternity he warned me never to engage in such an act again.

This was more than a relief to me. Thank God for the mercy of the instructor. I just went ahead and turned in my answers without answering the questions the student had helped me with. This was done to sooth my conscience, but it was very difficult to turn in my answers knowing that some of the questions were unanswered.

I felt foolish doing this and the thought of failing and maybe never graduating haunted me for a couple of days. Well, I had to do what I had to do. My feelings were wrong and my fears were baseless. The results were released and I passed French 102 with a C and went ahead to graduate with honors.

These two instances taught me not to allow my feelings to determine my actions. Feelings are not reliable, for they may change depending on circumstances surrounding you. Fear has the ability to cloud our judgment and cause us to make bad choices. Things are not always as dire as they appear to be.

If you allow predetermined principles of integrity and moral rectitude kick in, you will make the right choice when you are confronted with a choice between right and wrong. Making these right choices is not a onetime act, it is a lifestyle. We have to continuously and consciously remind ourselves to make the right choices when faced with conflicting propositions.

If it feels bad, it does not mean that we should not do it. Also, if it feels good it does not mean that we should go ahead and do it either. Our value system must be the inner compass that guides us. In my case the Word of God is my inner compass. Do I always make the right choice? The answer is no. But I made up my mind to do what is right no matter how costly it may be after these two instances. I have had to make many other choices after this instance. Some were good and some not so good.

I am still a work in progress, but getting better. That is why I refused to lie or fabricate stories that would enable me to be granted political asylum in the United States of America. It is one thing to decry the dictatorial regimes, embezzlement, corruption, and rigged elections in third world countries, Cameroon in particular. But to turn around and act in ways that are similar to those of the corrupt officials in power is not acceptable. Most of these dictatorial regimes are sustained by fear and lies.

The leaders are afraid to lose power and influence, so they override the constitution and the will of the people and become dictators. They lie to the people, for their promises are never kept. When the people express their wills through the ballot box, it is vehemently denied by the powers that be. They do this with the sole intent of maintaining their grip on power at the expense of the well-being of the entire country. Power is so important to them that no stone is left unturned by them to ensure that they are the only cocks that crow.

These leaders strengthen the military and the police. The forces of law and order that are supposed to serve the populace become the forces of lawlessness and disorder as they terrorize, brutalize, and exploit the very populace they are paid to defend and protect. In such a police state, fear abounds. The population cannot speak up, for if they do the strong arm of the military and the police will come down upon them. A lot of people end up in jail, some are killed, and others lose their jobs.

False charges are brought against these individuals by corrupt officials, and based on these lies, innocent citizens are sentenced by corrupt judges with impunity. There is no respect for the law. Right becomes wrong and wrong becomes right. Under such conditions the country is thrown into a moral crisis mode. People get into survival mode, fueled by fear and falsehood. "You have to do what you have to do to make ends meet" becomes the *modus operandi*.

Nothing becomes impossible, as we say in Cameroon, *"l' impossible n'est pas Camerounais."* This implies, for example, that if need be, you can forge your birth certificate and become younger if an opportunity requires you to be younger. This way of using temporal fixes to solve long-term problems has far-reaching implications on the entire system. No wonder the demographics are all mixed up. People who were supposed to retire are still working, but their performance is at its lowest. They reduced their ages and now they cannot deliver. This partially explains why the young, who are energetic with potential for greater productivity, are on the sidelines literally waiting for most of these older people to die on the job, for them to have a chance.

It becomes a herculean task for the country to maintain and update its infrastructure, and other basic social services. No wonder most of the African countries have almost given up. Their demographics are faulty and the way forward is cloudy and a maze of confusion. That is why after fifty years of independence, the death rate is still very high and the life expectancy is low.

This is not to imply that neo-colonialism has loosened its grip on the continent. I am not trying to make light of complicated issues here, but making the point that playing the blame card is part of the reason developing countries are where they are. Taking responsibility for our actions and taking the blame for our greed, selfishness, and self-centeredness will set us on the path to recovery. Blaming the outsiders and not holding our leaders accountable is a big mistake. The leaders have to learn to value their people and to ensure that better economic terms are negotiated with other countries. Instead they take kickbacks and hand over the natural resources of their countries on silver platters to multinational corporations.

It is difficult to negotiate deals with investors when a country does not have most of the technology and personnel to engage in capital-intensive ventures like exploring and exploiting natural resources. Who said being a leader was an easy job? It is a tough job to lead a nation and tough decisions have to be made that must benefit the entire country, not just a few. Instead, most of the leaders take the road of less resistance. They prefer cutting deals that will line their pockets with huge sums of money and fatten their foreign bank accounts.

It is not surprising that a politician from one of the oil-rich African countries was charged by British authorities for money laundering when a million pounds was found in his London house. A million British pounds is about 240 million Naira, the currency used in Nigeria. This

101

particular incident made international news headlines because the politician in question violated his bail terms by dressing in female clothes and escaping from Britain.

Money laundering, corruption, bribery, and plundering of public funds are hallmarks of dictatorial regimes. Those in power do all they can to stay in power, and their cohorts plunder the resources of the country with impunity. This results in suffering for a majority of the population where basic needs like access to clean water, good roads, and health care are nonexistent.

Many people escape from these dictatorial regimes and move to the West for a better life, and it seems natural for them to seek political asylum. This is okay, granted that they were involved in political struggles to free their country from oppressive regimes. But this is not always the case. Many people lie about their political activities in their countries of origin so that work papers can be given to them, usually driven by fear of missing the good life in the West.

Their rationale is to do all in their power to ensure that they gain employment in the West and send the much-needed remittances to their immediate families left behind under these dictatorial regimes. Their immediate concern is survival with little or no thought given to the implications of their actions. They do not care about painting a false image about their country for personal gain.

All of the negative publicity generated by such outlandish claims of torture and abuse that never occurred portrays an image of instability and a risky business environment for investors. It also discourages tourism, so most of the much-needed hard currency that tourist bring is lost, which worsens an already precarious situation, bringing more suffering on the entire nation.

This is not an issue of right or wrong. It is about developing a moral backbone. Whose morals apply here? The simple answer is: the same morals that are used to demand the politician to stop misappropriating and embezzling public funds. It is the same indignation that drives the public to demand truth from their leaders and ask for a fair share of the national cake.

Fear drives the leaders to cling to power at all cost. After close to three decades in power all these leaders know are the benefits of occupying those positions of leadership. They do not want to let go and will do all they can to stay there. How is this related to falsifying documents to get work papers? Fear of not having a job and other benefits that come with having work papers is the main motive. People who find themselves in this particular situation will do all they can to keep what they consider very important for their survival, just like the politician.

The cycle of fear and falsehood can be broken only when we develop a moral backbone. You no longer view your life from the point-of-view of what will benefit you as an individual, but factor in the impact of your actions on others. You start respecting and obeying the laws of God and those of man, knowing that breaking the law, even if you are not caught, will impact others negatively. You must understand that light and darkness do not mix, and that there is a distinction between good and evil. Lastly, doing wrong cannot make a right.

It is difficult to bring about change when, each time we are faced with difficulties, we let our inner compass adjust to the circumstances surrounding us. This is done by doing whatever it takes within our power to take advantage of the situation. If it means we cheat, lie, or steal, then so be it. This should not be so. We can do better. For example, those who initiated the wind of change that blew over most parts of Africa in the early 1960s and brought colonization to its knees were idealistic enough to preach that Africans could govern themselves.

Most of these individuals were faced with enormous tasks and challenges that seemed impossible to face, humanly speaking. But they refused to be selfish and considered the greater good above momentary satisfaction. Because of their courage and selflessness, they succeeded and achieved what many people told them was impossible. Our generation needs a new breed of sacrificial and selfless leaders armed with a strong moral backbone.

It appears more attractive to go with the flow and do what "everybody" is doing. After all, life is survival and when fire falls on you and your baby, you put out your own fire before attending to the needs of your baby. This sounds good and easy to do, but it not always the best thing to do.

Education and vibrant economies are not the solution to selfishness. Are the current leaders in Cameroon uneducated and poor? We will all say no. Why have they ruined our country and squandered our resources? Most of them studied in western countries, so what has prevented them from implementing what they learned from prestigious western educational institutions?

We have to face reality and the reality is that our country has been ravished by selfishness, hypocrisy, greed, and other vices, and the only way out is for us to change our survival strategies. Morality is not brought by economic or educational achievement, it is a personal decision and there is a cost associated with it. Most people are not willing to pay the price, so we have to pay the price in the long run to get out of the present quagmire.

This situation may appear hopeless, but there is hope we can make a difference by adhering to what is right and true. We cannot allow fear to rule our lives. Genuine change starts in the mind. It must result in adopting the right worldview and in being willing to pay the price when the time comes. This is not an easy endeavor. But it is doable.

I was in dire circumstances at the University of Texas at Dallas and there were few options that I could exploit. Since I was not making any money and there was no prospect for me to get a campus job or be made a teaching assistant, one of my first American friends, Shana, suggested I transfer to another school where I might be granted a teaching assistantship.

This friend was God-sent and a great encouragement to me. We were all in graduate school and taking an ore petrology class. She and another classmate invited me to the school cafeteria for lunch, and I thought, as was the practice in my country, that they were going to pay for the lunch. I was in for culture shock. They went ahead of me and ordered what they wanted, walked to the counter and paid, then went and sat down. I got my stuff and when I walked to the cashier, I was told that I had to pay for what I had ordered. I was barely getting by with little money and paying for that meal was more than a luxury. Thank God I had some money on me and was able to pay for it.

Despite this incident, I got to know and trust my new American friends and it turned out that our relationship would be a life-saver for me. Shana had graduated from the University of Texas at Arlington and proposed that I transfer there so that I might get a teaching assistantship. She drove me to the university campus and I dropped off my application. I did not have money for the application fee. What a relief that she took it upon herself to pay the application fee. While waiting to complete the application package at the University of Texas at Arlington, I continued taking classes at the University of Texas at Dallas.

CHAPTER 9

PUSHED AGAINST THE WALL

"Even though I walk through the darkest valley,
I will fear no evil, for you are with me; your rod and your staff,
they comfort me."

—Psalm 23:4

B Y DECEMBER 2002, I ran out of money completely. Throughout the entire semester, I prepared my food, ate out on very few occasions, and maintained a strict rationing of my meager resources. By the end of the semester my resources were gone. There was nothing to pay my rent with. That is when God intervened through Shana by using her to provide my rent for that month.

I was now at the end of my rope. There was no way for me to move forward. I had been able to patch through the first semester, but there was no way for me to continue patching. I needed a miracle to be able to go to school during the second semester. I could not envision how this was going to happen.

I had worked hard and made a couple of A grades during the first semester with a GPA of 3.68. I went again and talked with the head of the Geosciences Department about the need of a teaching assistantship or any help that could be offered, and I was told that my situation would be looked into, but no promises were made.

During the Christmas break, a cousin of mine came in one morning and told me that one of his friends, Scott, had a house that needed to be cleaned and suggested that we go do the cleaning. At last I was going to earn some money in America. The owner of the house was doing a remodeling job, and we had to strip wallpaper, paint, and clean the floors. At the end of the day $100 was handed to my cousin, and he gave me $20 and kept the rest. After all, he is the one who took me to his friend who needed help with his remodeling job. Twenty dollars might seem to be a small amount of money, but it was a lot to me.

Remember that by this time I had been in the United States for four months and had not earned a dime. This kept me from being able to send any money to my wife and son. I bought a phone card and called my wife and shared the good tidings with her. It was a great relief that I had finally made some money, but I was troubled that I was possibly breaking the law of the land.

Well, I reasoned that since I had offered help and was given something as compensation no wrong was committed. I had not asked to be paid any particular amount nor demanded my fair share of the money that was given to my cousin. Presumably, it appears I did such a good job helping my cousin's friend that he requested me to come back and help him again. We finally developed a friendship that is still ongoing. My friend picked me up one weekend and I spent all Saturday taking down wallpaper and stripping old tile from the floor. It was very cold, and suddenly I lifted up my eyes and realized that the yard and trees were all white. I moved closer to the door to see what was happening, and that was when I realized that a strange rain was falling. It was unlike the rain I had been used to. I went outside and put my hand out and thick white flakes fell on it, but were soon gone. I was experiencing my first snow in the northern hemisphere. Prior to coming to the United States of America, I had seen snow in movies, but the real thing took me completely by surprise.

When Scott came back at the end of the day to take me home, I asked him a ton of questions about what was going on. He was patient and kind enough to answer my questions. Whenever he took me to do something, he left me to work without supervision. He had noticed that there was something different about me and one day he told me that he had worked with people who would put in little effort when he was not present. I told him, God is my boss and that my first reward is from God; whatever my friend pays me is a plus. My Father in heaven is present at all times and whatever I do has to give Him glory.

It was a great relief to make a few dollars, but this was not enough to pay my tuition of more than $4,000. What was I to do? We kept praying and hoping that I would be able to go to school during the second semester. It was during this period that I was presented with another option to solve my problems: getting married to somebody who had permanent residency in the United States. This was the fastest way of getting legal papers and securing a good paying job in the United States of America.

Wow! What a solution and how attractive it seemed. Here I was, young and presumably single, and ready material for marriage. Let's say marriage of convenience. All of my problems would become history after I signed the marriage certificate. I was being presented with the silver bullet that would get me out of my predicament.

Who in their right minds would turn away from such a solution? Why would I want to keep living under pressure and seeming uncertainties? I alone had the answers to these questions. First, I had come to the U.S. to go to school, period, and making money was going to be a byproduct of being here and not the main purpose. Did I need the money? Definitely, but I would not allow fear to dictate how I approached the issue. Second, I was married and there was no way for me to get married again.

The plan was put forth for me to divorce my spouse and get married to some other woman, then later divorce that woman and remarry my spouse when she joins me in the future. Superficially, it made some sense, but my internal compass did not point in that direction. For it is written:

> "Haven't you read," he replied, "that at the beginning the Creator 'made them male and female,' and said, 'For this reason a man will leave his father and mother and be united to his wife, and the two will become one flesh'? So they are no longer two, but one flesh. Therefore what God has joined together, let no one separate." "Why then," they asked, "did Moses command that a man give his wife a certificate of divorce and send her away?" Jesus replied, "Moses permitted you to divorce your wives because your hearts were hard. But it was not this way from the beginning. I tell you that anyone who divorces his wife, except for sexual immorality, and marries another woman commits adultery."
>
> —Matthew 19:4–9

When I looked at the situation in light of this passage, it became apparent that the situation was a little more complicated than it appeared. I would be breaking God's law and my love for my Father in heaven would not permit me to do such a thing. Marriage is honorable and must be treated with utmost respect. It should not be reduced to a convenient arrangement for fictitious monetary gains. Divorcing my spouse would expose me to the possibility of committing adultery, telling lies, and digging a deeper hole than I could get out of.

It was during this period that I ran into somebody who had followed this process to get legal papers. One afternoon, I boarded a DART (Dallas Area Transit) bus on my way to the Arapaho train station to get onboard the train to Dallas. On my way, I got into a conversation with the bus driver. I figured out that since he was African-American he might be able to offer me some good advice. I quickly learned that one has to be careful and cautious when seeking counsel.

I asked him what his country of origin was and how he got his job. He told me that when he arrived in the United States of America from Ghana a few years before, he had no legal papers to work, but "God" in his mercy provided somebody who was willing to organize a fake marriage with him. He did not actually marry this lady, but they signed a marriage certificate and divorced after he got his papers. I had heard these stories from people who said they knew of other people who had used this method to get papers, but I had not yet had an encounter with somebody who had done it.

Here was my opportunity to get the story from the horse's mouth. It was somehow difficult to believe that this guy had done this and saw nothing wrong with his actions. By the way, why was I having this conversation with him just at the time of my greatest need for legal papers? Was he some sort of a messenger to help me out of my predicament?

From all indications the guy was very happy with the decision he had made and life was being good to him. He had papers and a job that was bringing in some money. Unlike me, who had nothing to show. It was getting very close to the beginning of the second semester and I had not yet heard from the Geosciences Department. I needed some sort of solution badly; legal papers, a job, anything that would help me. Maybe this was my opportunity for firsthand information that might shed some light on my situation.

I pressed the guy a little more about the moral grounds of getting married to get papers, and he said he was raised by Christian parents. In fact, his parents were elders in the particular denomination that he was raised in. I was impressed and comforted that this is someone who was supposedly led by the same internal compass as I was.

However, I was shocked when he said there was nothing wrong with arranging a fake marriage to get papers. I could not wrap my mind around what he said. He dropped the bomb when he suggested that "God" would provide someone who would willingly do that for me. God? We were at the bus station and I had to get off the bus. I lamely told the guy that I would not do such a thing and he made me to understand that I was not realistic enough and that the road ahead of me was going to be a difficult one. He was right, the road has been

111

a very difficult one, but you would not be holding this book if I had gone the other way!

As difficult as it may be, who said life was a bed of roses? Who said the absence of trials is an indication that all is well? Did Jesus not talk about denying ourselves? Did He not talk about us carrying our cross on a daily basis?

> Then he said to them all: "whoever wants to be my disciple must deny himself and take up his cross daily and follow me. For whoever wants to save his life will lose it, but whoever loses his life for me will save it. What good is it for someone to gain the whole world, and yet lose or forfeit his very self?"
>
> —Luke 9:23–25

The cross signifies discomfort, suffering, shame, rejection, pain, and death. Carrying our cross is more than wearing a little ornament around our neck, it must be from the inside and our outward actions should attest to that. If we carry our cross, we will die to our own agenda and will finally get to a place where we stop trying to help God, but allow God to help us. This is a lonely place and you may be misunderstood and ridiculed by those you think would support you.

My conversation with the driver on the bus left me scratching my head for some answers. My convictions ran contrary to my predicament. I was badly in need of resources to sustain my life. To make matters worse, the money I had borrowed from the money lenders was accruing at 10% per month and by January 2003, interest alone was $300 a month. Was I ever going to get out of this debt? Where could I turn? Even the church I was attending seemed to have little to offer. Should I say I was disillusioned by their reaction to my situation? Should I turn to the church I was attending for help?

As was the tradition in the Full Gospel Mission in Cameroon, each time you travel you get letters of recommendations from your pastor and hand it to the next pastor in the new church you attend. Therefore,

I came to the U.S. armed with a couple of recommendation letters. When I settled in a church here in the U.S. on the recommendation of my missionary friend, I set up an appointment with the senior pastor of the church and handed him my recommendation letter. I shared with him about the challenges I was facing.

Here I was six months later and had not had any feedback from the church. Where was I to turn? God is the person taking care of us and we have to depend on Him and Him alone at all times. Man will fail us and we dare not put our trust or confidence in any man or system.

I understand this particular church was going through a major restructuring venture. They were about to sell their present church building and buy a bigger one. It needed an extra $2 million dollars for the deal to be finalized. The pastor exhorted the church congregation for quite some months to trust God to provide the $2 million. He needed everybody on board for the project to be realized. I would sit in church during these sermons and play the figures in my mind. This congregation had more than one hundred members. If it was that hard for them to take on a debt of $2 million, what about me taking on a larger personal debt? I owed three million francs. It is difficult to compare apples and oranges. This did not make it easier on me though. All I could do was to trust my Father in heaven and keep reminding Him that He had a debt to pay and that I was waiting to see how He was going to pay it.

CHAPTER 10

BREAKTHROUGH AT LAST

"And without faith it is impossible to please God, because anyone who comes to him must believe that he exists and that he rewards those who earnestly seek him."

—Hebrews 11:6

THEN CAME JANUARY 2003, a new semester was about to start without any money for me to register. I just had to wait and trust God for a miracle. What was the probability that I would get a teaching assistantship? The odds were against me. This was the start of the spring semester and budgets for the school year are approved at the beginning of the fall semester.

Therefore, it was going to take an extraordinary arrangement to secure a teaching assistantship for me that would enable me to pay my rent, food, and clothes, and to remain in school. If this does not happen, I would have to go back to Cameroon. Could I really afford to go back?

My return ticket had just expired and even if I went back, what would I do with the three million francs debt that I owed? In fact, another Christian leader had suggested that I go back home, pay off my debts, and then come back to study. I will not blame him for thinking like that, but if he had a clue of where I was coming from he would have offered a more practical solution. I was also homesick and missing my wife, son, and family. It felt like we would never set eyes on each other again. I was too far from home, communication was very expensive, and there wasn't enough money to keep in touch on a consistent basis.

I kept checking my mailbox to see if the department head had offered me a teaching assistantship. I checked and checked and the days drew closer and closer for classes for the spring semester to start and there was nothing. Something must happen for me to go to school in the spring. God has to come through for me somehow.

Finally, one blessed Sunday evening I went to check my mailbox and there it was—a letter signed by the head of the department, stating that I had been offered a teaching assistantship position. "Praise the Lord!" I shouted. I then went on my knees in the student lounge and offered a prayer of praise to God.

The miracle was now a reality. It had been a very long wait, but the wait was over. Tears of joy and gratitude began to stream down my cheeks. Yes! Yes! Yes! I was going to stay in school. I was going to have money to pay my rent. I would have some to send to my spouse and son and we would even be able to start paying off the three million francs I owed. Such great joy and gratitude flooded my soul. This was nothing short of a miracle. I would be made to understand a few months later, while trying to bring my spouse and son over, that some special arrangement had been made for me to get the teaching assistantship and that it could be taken away if things went wrong in the Geosciences Department. This is the subject of another book.

At the same time, I was still glowing from what the Lord had done and praising my Father in heaven for such a wonderful breakthrough. My joy, however, was going to be short-lived. The debt that we owed was threatening to undo all that the Lord had done. My teaching assistantship package came with free tuition, but I still had to pay for books and other things. This meant paying off the debt, and bringing my spouse and son to live with me in the U.S. was still far-fetched.

116

How in the world was I going to pay off the debt when the interest at this point was $300 per month and growing? My TA stipend at this point was a little above $1,000 per month. Paying off just the interest of $300 per month on the debt, my rent, food, and other things would leave me with little or nothing.

I figured out that the best thing to do was to send as much money as possible to Cameroon towards the repayment of the debt. By the third month, which was March 2003, I figured out that no matter how much I struggled it would take many years for me to pay off the debt. I felt trapped and needed help. Once in a while, I would take up a calculator and compute how much I needed each month and how long it was going to take for me to pay off the debt, and each time the prognosis was disheartening. In addition to this, the owners of the money were pressuring me to pay off the debt.

I tried to explain the circumstances surrounding me to them, but they would not listen. I was made to understand that there was money in the U.S. and that I should work hard to pay off the debt. Working hard was out of the question. It was impossible to work and go to school because I had no work papers. There comes a time when there is nothing you can do to change the circumstances surrounding you. The only viable option is to trust, pray, and wait.

How could I blame them? Their money had been a lifesaver and without it I would not have been in the U.S. in the first place. This money was given to me without any collateral security. This help came from people who did not even know me. My church family that I depended on and hoped would help me was unable to do so. I had contacted some elders and shared with them what my need was, but nothing was done. When we pray God answers our prayers in His own time and in His own way. God chooses who to use to deliver the answer to our prayer. We have to remove our eyes from people and focus on God.

Focusing on God, and not on people, will spare us the pain that comes from being let down by the people we trust and depend on. People will always be people and most of the time they will not respond to your predicament in the way you expect. This is one of the most valuable lessons I learned. Trust the Lord to make a way and let Him do it in His own way and at His timing. It is difficult to do this, especially when you are surrounded by relatives and well-to-do loved ones who are in a better position to help, but opt not to. Instead of developing bitterness and resentment towards them, understand that God might not have elected to answer your prayer through them.

God is forever your source and you have to completely depend on Him. The common reaction is to blame those you expected help from for not helping. It is left to these particular individuals to let God answer your prayer through them. If they refuse to let God use them, God will raise other people. Nobody can prevent God from fulfilling His promises in your life. God has the ability to use the very things that appear to be obstacles to move you to the next step towards the fulfillment of your dream.

Joseph shared his dreams of becoming a leader with his brothers and out of jealousy they sold him to slave drivers. His new master placed him in charge of his business. This enabled Joseph to learn administrative skills and management skills that would later on become very handy when he became the prime minister of Egypt. With time Joseph excelled as a business manager, but his master's wife tried to seduce him to commit adultery. What a perfect solution for him to solve his problem of being a slave. Maybe having sex with his master's wife could have bought his freedom, but Joseph refused to sin against God.

This decision to do what was right landed Joseph in prison. This is a clear indication that bad things can happen to good people, but the good news is that God has the ability to make something great out of the bad things. In Joseph's case, the prison, which was definitely "a bad thing," brought him in contact with high-ranking Egyptian officials, whose dreams he interpreted. Eventually Joseph had free publicity from one of the high-ranking officials when the time was ripe.

God's timing and the manner in which He does things is impeccable. There are no delays and no missed opportunities when we walk in His will. Pharaoh, the king of Egypt, had a troubling dream and all his magicians were clueless as to what the meaning of the dream was. There was a great need for an interpretation of this dream. That was when one of the high-ranking officials who had been in prison with Joseph remembered him. This official told Pharaoh about Joseph and he was immediately brought out of prison and presented before Pharaoh. God used Joseph to interpret the dream. Subsequently, Pharaoh made Joseph the second-in-command in Egypt. As you can see, even the prison could not prevent Joseph's dream from coming to pass.

Now that I was earning some money, I thought it would be easy to borrow some money from friends in the U.S. and use this money to pay off the debt that was at 10% interest a month, a total of 120% a year.

That is when I found out that, true to the words of my friend as expressed in the letter that was sent to me, "In America we have to work hard for the money we get … it looks as if everyone is prosperous, but the majority are struggling to make ends meet and everyone is working to pay the bills." This is the typical response I got. "We do not have money." "We have to pay our bills." "Do not expect any help from us."

Since I was not successful in getting money from anybody, I went to the bank. What a crazy idea. What was I thinking? What bank in their right mind was going to give me a loan without me first establishing that I had an excellent credit history and that I was credible enough to pay back the money? I told the banker that I was making more than one thousand dollars a month. He ran the numbers and told me I would not be given a loan. My only chance, he said, was to get someone to cosign the loan. Someone to cosign the loan? I pondered. There was nobody who was going to cosign the loan for me.

I had to save as much as possible so that I would become debt free. Therefore, I did not get a car or a phone. It would take me a year to finally get a landline. I was moving around on a bicycle that Dr. Collins had given to me. This is how I came close to being killed by a distracted driver one fateful morning on my way home from the bank.

At the end of each month, I rode my bicycle for about two and a half miles to the bank to collect my salary, and then I wired money by MoneyGram® to Cameroon for my debts to be paid. This particular morning in March 2003, I was riding my bike on the far right-hand side of the road on Coit. Coit Road is quite busy in the morning, but, being new in the U.S., I was not familiar with the area to take a less busy road. There I was, having a nice morning ride. I had already collected my money that morning and was about half a mile from the bank. When I approached the intersection between Coit Road and Arapaho Road I immediately crossed the intersection and I heard a noise behind me.

There was no time to turn, or to assess what was going on. Suddenly, a car appeared on my left-hand side and hit me. What was going on? Was I going to die? I was not even wearing a helmet. The car brushed me on the left-hand side and I crashed onto the road. My greatest fear was that the car was going to climb over me. Thank God the car did not drive over me. I hit the road hard and my bicycle took quite a beating. I thought I was not going to get up. I was expecting to see blood all over the road and some serious injuries. Surprisingly, I got up and there was nothing seriously wrong with me. I felt a little pain from a slight bruise on my face and that was it.

The car that pushed me stopped a few feet away and an elderly lady got out of the car. I was wondering, "How on earth, I almost got killed by her car." So I asked her if she did not see me. She said she did not see me, and went on to tell me that she was rushing to the airport to pick somebody up. I could not believe what I was hearing.

How could she not see me? I was wearing a red jacket and riding as far to the edge of the road as possible. The lady was very sympathetic and insisted that I go to the hospital and see a doctor. I told her I was okay and would not go to any hospital. Before you blame me for not going for a medical checkup and calling the police, etc., factor in the fact that I was new in the U.S. and did not know what to do.

You will be surprised to hear that on one occasion I could not cross a major street because I thought I would be breaking the law. One hot afternoon, about three weeks after my arrival, I left the university campus to get a few things from Albertsons. Going to the grocery store meant I had to cross a couple of streets. After crossing the first minor street, I came to a double lane street and stood by the road for some time.

Cars kept passing and passing, with occasional breaks. I looked east and west and there was no one across the road. I was more than surprised. In my country at any given moment in our cities there are more people on the streets than cars. Here it was the opposite, lots of cars on the road but nobody waiting or trying to cross the street. I thought crossing the road on foot was committing a crime, and not wanting to get into trouble I made a u-turn and went back to the university campus. A friend gave me a ride later on for me to go get what I needed from the grocery store. I shared with him what had transpired earlier, and he could not hold back the laughter. I have since laughed at myself each time I think about this.

You can imagine my apprehension when the lady knocked me down with her car. I did not want to get into any trouble and did not want to get this poor lady into trouble either. I did not even take the lady's license or telephone numbers, or any other information. I just told her I was okay, got on my battered bike, and rode home.

When I got to the apartment, I told my roommates about the accident and one of them told me that I was going to get rich. I asked, "How?" He explained to me that I needed to get a lawyer and follow up so that the lady's insurance company would pay me some money. His idea was attractive, for I needed money badly.

Despite this, I told the roommate that it was not necessary to go through all that, since I had not sustained any injuries and was fine. He said, "Eric, man, you will never get rich again in this country. You just let a golden opportunity to slip through your fingers." It seemed I had lost my only chance to get out of my debts. I just had to push the thought of pursuing the kind elderly lady to get money to pay off my debts out of my mind. This was not easy, though. I kept having this nagging question: "Don't you think God wants to use this accident to answer your prayer?" I finally figured out that God did not want me to pay the debt through this means.

I had told God that He owed it, and that He had to figure out a way to pay off the debt. I kept reminding Him, and all I could do was just to wait for Him to do it in His own way and at His timing.

I had shared my struggles with Dr. James Carter, a geology professor at the University of Texas at Dallas, a few months before and he had said that he would see what he could do. Sometime in February he gave me some forms to apply for a scholarship. He asked me how much the debt was and told me that he was going to try and get enough money so that the scholarship would pay the entire balance of my debt. I went ahead and filled out the application forms and handed them to him. I called my wife and informed her of the latest developments. We prayed and kept our fingers crossed.

Sometime in March, Dr. Carter informed me that the scholarship had been approved. This scholarship was awarded by the Southwest Section of the Society for Mining, Metallurgy, and Exploration (SME). I was invited to a Mexican restaurant for a special dinner in my honor. It was difficult to express my joy and gratitude for this scholarship. This was more than a lifesaver to me. When I accepted the scholarship, the award committee asked me if the money was enough to pay off my debts. I said yes. In fact the money was more than enough. I had a small balance left after paying the entire debt.

This was a miracle and my Father in heaven had honored His word. He had paid off the debt. This scholarship was unique in that it specified that I could pay off my debt with it. This was not the norm. In most cases graduate scholarships are awarded to students to do research, not pay debts. At least, that was my experience throughout the rest of graduate school. I did not get any other scholarships to pay debts. I applied for other research grants, but was not too successful. This is why I believe that God provided money to pay off the debt through Dr. James Carter and the scholarship committee.

I learned that God uses whoever He chooses and that all we have to do is to wait for His timing. For God's time is the best and He is never late.

I was finally debt free and ready to focus on my graduate studies. At last, I felt that God had indeed asked me to come to the U.S. for graduate studies because, so far, He had been very instrumental in guiding me and providing for my needs. My dependence on Him deepened and my faith became stronger. The strengthening of my faith was vital to me, for a lot of challenges were still ahead of me; coming to America was just the beginning of my journey of faith. But I was confident that, God who brought me to America was going to keep me and grant me success.

University housing at the University of Texas at Dallas. My apartment was on the third floor and was quite an upgrade from my housing during undergraduate studies in Cameroon.

Dr. Duane Collins and his wife, Ruth, at my graduation. Dr. Collins picked me up at the airport and helped with the initial transition into life in America.

124

More than eight years later, God has increased our family. Elizabeth and myself (Eric) are the adults, and from left to right: Abeutmboma (2), Ntsongmboma (6), Afaamboma (9), and Elotmboma (4).

With Dr. James Carter at the oral examination of my doctoral thesis at the Geosciences Department, University of Texas at Dallas

EPILOGUE

THE CALL TO walk by faith is not a onetime deal; it is a lifestyle of continuous trust in, and obedience to God's Word. All of my debt was paid, but my journey was far from over. It was just the beginning of life in America for me. My faith needed to be stronger, for there was still a lot ahead of me. My wife and son were still in Cameroon. A special arrangement had been made for me to become a teaching assistant. Would this arrangement hold? Would I be able to support my family on a student stipend? Would I have enough resources to finish graduate school? The list of questions went on and on.

Fortunately, I knew where to get the answers to these questions. I had to once more turn to my Father in heaven for guidance and support. All I have been through up to this point was adequate preparation for what was ahead of me. Coming to America was a walk of faith and living in America is still going to be a walk of faith.

During the next couple of years, I will have to affirm time and again that the circumstances surrounding me cannot limit what God can do in my life. I have seen Him do great miracles in my life, and I have the assurance and confidence that He is still in the miracle business and that He will see me and my family through.

God made it possible for me to be reunited with my wife and son after exactly one year, as we had prayed. We defied all conventional wisdom, by my wife and our young son joining me in the United States of America. I was a student with a very small income and conventional wisdom was for me to leave my family in Cameroon and only bring them after graduating and securing a well-paying job.

Not only did my wife come, we went ahead and had three other children, while both of us were students. It took the special grace of God and numerous divine interventions for us to handle school and a growing family. It is not fun when you are forced out of your house and made to move into a bigger house because your family size has changed, while your income does not change to catch up with your expanding needs. All in all, we saw the faithfulness of God and the names of our children bear a testament of what God has done in our lives.

Our first son is named Afaamboma, which means "God's work" or "the Lord's doing" in the Mundani language. Indeed, the Lord had done it and we got married with little resources. The Lord reunited the family and we had a baby girl and named her Ntsogmboma, which means "God's favor." It was His favor for my spouse and son to join me in the U.S. after a year of separation. The entire story of what transpired next is in the next book that is in the works.

Two years later, God blessed us with another girl and we named her Elotmboma, which means "God's blessing." Yes, God blessed us in a foreign land and met our needs. He provided enough funds for me to go through graduate school, and I graduated with a doctorate in geosciences from the University of Texas at Dallas, debt free. All that transpired through graduate school is the subject of the next book: *Living in America: A Journey of Faith.*

Our greatest concern close to graduation was getting a job for me. As an international student, I needed a company that would sponsor me to get a temporary work permit, called an H1B visa and it requires the company willing to offer the job to hire attorneys to file for the candidate.

There are other fees that have to be paid to the Department of Homeland Security by the company, making this process an expensive one. Because of this, many companies do not like sponsoring international students if they can find American students or students with permanent residence status.

This meant that the search for a job was going to be a challenging one. An already difficult situation was compounded by the fact that I had not done an internship during my graduate studies. Despite all of these setbacks, the Lord answered our prayers and provided me with a job before I graduated.

A little less than a year after graduation God blessed us with another baby girl and we named her Abeutmboma, which means "God answers." The Lord had answered our prayer and provided a job. Now we were ready to start a new life in Denver, Colorado.

Having a job and relocating to Denver, Colorado, opened yet another chapter in our walk of faith and brought its own challenges. All we had done to that point was just to trust and obey. Life has to be lived one day at a time. As the writer John Sammis of my favorite hymn says:

When we walk with the Lord
in the light of His word,
what a glory He sheds on our way!
While we do His good will,
He abides with us still,
and with all who will trust and obey.

Chorus/Refrain
Trust and obey, for there's no other way
to be happy in Jesus, but to trust and obey.

Not a burden we bear,
not a sorrow we share,
but our toil he doth richly repay;
not a grief or a loss,
not a frown or a cross,
but is blest if we trust and obey.

Chorus/Refrain

But we never can prove
the delights of His love
until all on the altar we lay;
for the favor He shows,
for the joy He bestows,
are for them who will trust and obey.

Chorus/Refrain

Then in fellowship sweet
we will sit at His feet,
or we'll walk by His side in the way;
what He says we will do,
where He sends we will go;
never fear, only trust and obey.

"Trusting the Lord to see us through each day." *John H. Sammis,
1846–1919*

BIOGRAPHY

Dr. Eric Tayem Tangumonkem holds a Bachelor's degree in Geology and a minor in Sociology from the University of Buea in Cameroon, a Master's in Earth Sciences from the University of Yaounde in Cameroon, and a Doctorate in Geosciences from the University of Texas at Dallas. In addition to being a Geoscientist at Denbury Resources, he is a poet, an inspirational/motivational speaker, and President/co-founder of IEM APPROACH LLC., IEM Press and Equipping of the Saints International Ministries based in Dallas, Texas. He is married to Elizabeth and God has blessed them with four children: Afaamboma, Nstongmboma, Elotmboma, and Abuetmboma.

Now that you have been blessed, encouraged and your faith strengthened by the testimony in this book. You should pass the blessings to others by doing one or all of the following:

- Order extra copies of the book for your family members, friends and colleagues
- Share what you have learned from the book with others
- Invite Dr. Tangumonkem to come share his motivational/inspirational message with your family, friends and colleagues

Dr. Tangumonkem is available to share his testimony in churches, schools, social events etc.

Phone: 214-908-3963
Web: www.erictangumonkem.com
E-mail: et@erictangumonkem.com

Part of the proceeds from the sales of this book are being used to support orphans at HOTPEC orphanage located in Mile 15 Bokova, South West Region Cameroon

IEM PRESS

Inspire, Motivate & Equip

To order additional copies of this book call:
214-908-3926
or visit our website at
www.iempublishing.com

If you enjoyed this quality custom-published book,
drop by our website for more books and information.

"Inspiring, Equipping and Motivating Publishing"

Lightning Source UK Ltd.
Milton Keynes UK
UKOW02f0046150115

244478UK00002B/49/P